M000084111

Overflowing
FULLNESS

A Journey into the Father's Heart

Kierra Blaser

WestBow
PRESS
A DIVISION OF THOMAS NELSON

Copyright © 2011 by Kierra Blaser

All rights reserved. No part of this book may be used or reproduced by any means, graphic, electronic, or mechanical, including photocopying, recording, taping or by any information storage retrieval system without the written permission of the publisher except in the case of brief quotations embodied in critical articles and reviews.

Scripture taken from the Holy Bible, New International Version®. Copyright © 1973, 1978, 1984 Biblica. Used by permission of Zondervan. All rights reserved.

Scripture taken from the Amplified Bible, *Copyright © 1954, 1958, 1962, 1964, 1965, 1987 by The Lockman Foundation. Used by permission.*

WestBow Press books may be ordered through booksellers or by contacting:

WestBow Press
A Division of Thomas Nelson
1663 Liberty Drive
Bloomington, IN 47403
www.westbowpress.com
1-(866) 928-1240

ISBN: 978-1-4497-2427-6 (sc)
ISBN: 978-1-4497-2429-0 (hc)
ISBN: 978-1-4497-2428-3 (e)

Library of Congress Control Number: 2011914745

Because of the dynamic nature of the Internet, any web addresses or links contained in this book may have changed since publication and may no longer be valid. The views expressed in this work are solely those of the author and do not necessarily reflect the views of the publisher, and the publisher hereby disclaims any responsibility for them.

Any people depicted in stock imagery provided by Thinkstock are models, and such images are being used for illustrative purposes only.

Certain stock imagery © Thinkstock.

Printed in the United States of America

WestBow Press rev. date: 11/17/2011

Contents

In honor of my dear friend and hero, Betty Teka –

You understood the overflowing heart of the Father better than anyone I know, and your overflowing life of fullness was one of the most beautiful and contagious that I've seen. Thank you for walking in the joy of knowing that you're "His favorite," and reminding each of us that we too are "His favorites." I look forward to dancing with you for all eternity.

Acknowledgements

Thank you to the countless friends and family who helped make this book possible.

Christy, thank you for the love you poured into editing this book. What a gift to have an editor who understands my heart so deeply. I couldn't have done this without you.

Mom, Dad, Kristen, and my amazing grandparents, thank you for believing in me, encouraging me, and helping fund this project. I love you.

Leah, thank you for your love, encouragement, and the picture for the cover (www.visphotography.com).

Michael, my incredible husband, thank you for your contagious passion for the fullness of God. Thank you for creating a culture in our home that treasures and invites God's overflowing fullness. Thank you for encouraging me to live this message each day. There is no one I'd rather walk this journey with.

Heavenly Father, thank you for inviting me on this journey with you. Thank you for so tenderly sharing your heart with me and entrusting these words to me. I am honored and humbled.

Preface: Learning to Breathe

It was a sunny afternoon in the beautiful village of Kipkaren, Kenya, but the forecast in my heart wasn't matching the weather outside. While the sun shone brightly through the window of my hut, my soul felt dreary and foggy. I was tired. Not with a sleepy tiredness that an hour nap would cure; no, this was a deep-down-soul-tiredness.

Here I was living my dream in the country that had captured my heart—watching orphans placed in families, the sick cared for, and the poor empowered—but my service felt lifeless and my soul exhausted. *What's going on Lord?* I asked as I lay on the bed of my hut. I knew I needed to spend some time in His presence seeking His wisdom and help. *Why do I feel so tired in the depths of my soul?* I waited quietly on Him to answer.

After a few minutes, He placed a picture in my mind of a girl singing on stage. She was singing quite beautifully and receiving much praise from the crowd, but all the power for her singing was coming from her throat. Now I am definitely not a singer (that was one gift that didn't get mixed into my family gene pool), but I do know that singers are supposed to sing by using their diaphragms, not their throats. I've heard that if you sing from your throat, your vocal chords will get tired and strained and eventually wear out.

"Kierra," I heard the Father gently whisper, "you're tired and worn out because you've been 'singing from your throat' for the last 20 years. This is not how I created you to 'sing' for me. It's time to learn to sing from your diaphragm—to sing from your core. Otherwise, you're not going to last for the long haul."

The picture made perfect sense and I knew God was right. I had been 'singing from my throat': living, ministering, and loving out of my own strength—striving to work *for* Him instead of abiding *in* Him and living from that place of intimacy.

Thankful to have a clear picture of what was going on, I began to wonder, *how does one sing using one's diaphragm?* I knew I needed to live and minister from a deeper place, to draw from a power and source deeper than my own, but I wasn't quite sure how to make the switch. Luckily, I have a friend Joshua who is an amazing singer and was able to provide me with some valuable insight:

> Yes, it is true. Singers must sing from their diaphragm (or stomach); otherwise, their voice will tire and go hoarse, and may eventually disappear and/or be permanently damaged. When I started singing, the first thing my voice teacher focused on was learning to use my diaphragm: the 'foundation of singing' as she called it. You start by breathing deeply—so deeply that the stomach feels like it is filled with air. Many people suppose it's the clenching or squeezing of the stomach muscles, but it's actually the releasing of them to allow everything to expand, like a tire all the way around your stomach. It's easy to do the front part, but it has to expand in the back too. My teacher would often put her hands on my back to check to see if I was breathing correctly.

Once a singer begins to breathe correctly, they can use the diaphragm to help with singing. It's like a motor—once it's started, it propels itself and they'll feel like they can sing forever. As they continue to use the diaphragm, they'll be able to sing higher, louder, and longer and will have more control over dynamics and artistic phrasing. It's really different from throat singing and when they finally get it, they'll know it.

I was amazed by his response and knew it was time to learn to breathe deeper spiritually. It was time to soak in God's presence until He was completely filling me, and then live from that place of fullness. I wanted to begin to live from my core, from the place where God's very presence dwelt within me. I wanted Jesus to radically capture my heart, take it over, make it fully alive, and then live from *that* place!

So I decided to stop a lot of my 'throat singing' for God (my service and work for Him) to make room for God to lead me into a season of 'breathing exercises'. I knew I needed time to simply *be* with Him to allow Him to teach me to live from a different source. This was crucial. As Joshua shared, breathing is the 'foundation of singing' and I wanted my spiritual foundation with the Lord to be solid.

This book is the fruit of what God taught me as I learned to 'breathe' and live from a deeper place with Him. It is the conversation I had with Him as I began to sit at His feet each day. I would ask Him questions, close my eyes at the computer, listen with my spirit, and write. I wasn't used to listening to God like this, but as I took time to be still with Him, I began to realize how much He wanted to share with me. Though I didn't hear an audible voice, when everything inside of me was quiet and focused on Him, I heard a 'voice' separate from my own, a 'voice' I knew was God's.

As I listened to His voice, I grew to deeply know and trust this God who desires intimacy with us more than anything else, the One who comes to share the depth of His heart with us as we take time to listen. Sometimes God shares with us through the Bible—His love letter to us. Other times, His Holy Spirit gives us impressions and words. However God chooses to speak, one thing is for sure—He loves to reveal Himself to us and has sent His own Spirit to live in us to counsel, guide and teach us. He is a personal God who is all about relationship, and relationship requires conversation.

I didn't know initially that this would become something others would read. But as I recorded this conversation in my journal, I sensed God asking me to invite others into it, because His words are for them too. So, at His prompting, I share these words with you and pray that He speaks to you as you come near to listen with me. Welcome to my conversation with God!

Introduction

As I stepped into this season of 'learning to breathe' correctly, God centered my breathing lessons on the theme of fullness: the fullness of His heart for me and the fullness He created me to live in each day. More than anything, He desired for me to understand the truth of His overflowing heart and to step into the overflowing life for which I was created. These two themes make up the two parts of this book.

As you read through the different sections, I encourage you to read slowly, listen with your spirit, and take the time to do the 'breathing exercises' at the end of each reading. This book wasn't meant to be read quickly. If you read it fast, you will likely miss the depth of what God wants to say to you. Take your time and practice the breathing exercises. I encourage you to go through one reading per day, or even one reading per week. I invite you to learn to breathe with me through these lessons, that together we might begin to truly grasp the goodness of His overflowing heart and enter the fullness for which we were created!

I pray that as you read my conversation with God, it will encourage you to dive deeper into your own conversation with Him. I pray that as you listen to His generous, overflowing heart, it will give you courage to ask Him your own questions. These were simply His words to me, but you might be dealing with different situations that need their own answers from Him. So as you read, ask for a revelation of the truth of God's heart for you and wait on Him until He brings it. He loves sharing His heart with His children and delights to communicate with us. So let's come near; let's listen; let's receive; and let's become people rooted and established in His love—a love that causes us to blossom into the overflowing, life-giving masterpieces He created us to be.

PART 1

HIS OVERFLOWING HEART

The Fullness of His Heart

*"Blessed is the man who **trusts in the You** [leaning and believing on You, committing all and **confidently looking to You**, and that without fear or misgiving]!"*
Psalm 84:12 Amplified Bible

A few days after my conversation with God about my need to live from a deeper place, I once again found myself crying out to Him from my little hut in Kipkaren, Kenya. This time it had to do with the issue of trust . . .

Lord, I'm so frustrated. Why is it that after walking with you for over twenty years, I still have trouble trusting you with certain areas of my life? I want to 'trust you with all my heart and lean not on my own understanding,'[1] but sometimes that's so hard for me. I want to confidently lean on you and look to you in every circumstance without fear or misgiving,[2] but I don't always know how. I want to trust you for a husband; to trust that you care about that desire in my heart and are able and willing to fill it. But it seems impossible to me right now. Here I am in the middle of this tiny village, and I just don't see any potential Prince Charmings coming my way. Lord, where is he going to come from? I want to trust you with all my heart and rest in complete confidence in you in every situation, but that's just not my reality right now. Why can't I fully trust you? What's getting in the way?

---

[1] Proverbs 3:5
[2] Psalms 84:12

3

"Beloved, the problem is that you don't fully know or believe my heart for you. You will never fully trust someone without knowing their heart and intentions towards you. In order to trust me with complete confidence, you must first understand my heart for you.

I understand your struggle. I see the past disappointments, wounds, and pain—the times that you've felt let down by me and by others. I know every seed of doubt the enemy has planted in your heart and every lie that he's spoken to you. I know it all. But today I want to give you a revelation of the truth of my heart for you and redeem and rescue all of your insecurities, wounds, and doubts."

Oh thank you Lord! You're right, I don't understand the truth of your heart for me, but I desperately want to. Please share it with me—I'm listening.

"Beloved, this is my heart for you; this is what is true:

I long for you to experience abundant, overflowing life.
I desire for my joy to be in you and for your joy to be complete.
I delight in and am delighted by you.
I will never withhold any good thing from you.
I take pleasure in giving you the desires of your heart.
I love lavishing my generosity on you.
I long to overflow your cup.
I am committed to your wholeness.
I desire for you to radiate my love and glory."

Tears came to my eyes as I heard these words straight from my Father. They seemed almost too good to be true. Could His heart really overflow with this much love, delight, and goodness for me? My head believed Him, but my heart remained skeptical.

It definitely hadn't always *felt* like these things were true. And yet, something deep within me knew that there was a truth in His words far deeper than anything I felt.

I longed for the truth of His words to be the biggest reality I lived in. I yearned to understand everything He meant when He spoke of abundant life, complete joy, and an overflowing cup. I realized that after walking with Him for twenty years, I still didn't understand the depth of these concepts and the grandness of His love. I didn't want to miss out anymore. I didn't want to live another day outside of this revelation of His overflowing heart for me!

The season that followed was an exhilarating journey of mining the depths of each of these statements. I dug into the scriptures, asked questions, listened to His Spirit, and began to fall madly in love with the most generous, passionate, and beautiful heart I've ever known. The following chapters are a compilation of what I discovered on that journey.

* *Breathing Exercises:*

1. *What is the hardest area of your life to trust God with? Why is that? Carve out some time to bring this area before the Lord. Share your feelings honestly with Him. Share your doubts, confusion, and pain. And then after sharing your heart with Him, ask Him to share His. Quiet yourself and listen from your spirit. Let Him share the truth of His heart and character with you. Write down anything He says to you. Don't worry about trying to figure out if what you are hearing is really from Him. If you have invited Him to be the Lord of your life, His Spirit is living in you and does speak to you. So write down anything you hear or sense in your spirit (it may come as a strong impression, or a clear thought suddenly*

5

in your mind, or words that seem to come from deep within your spirit). And if you don't have a relationship with God yet, He's excited to speak to you as well and to invite you into a conversation. If you don't hear or sense anything from Him at first, don't worry. You will continue to learn to recognize His voice throughout this book. He will respond to you and you will hear from Him on this journey.

2. *Re-read His words in this section. These are His words to you. Soak in them for a bit. Let them sink in. Which of these truths about His heart is hardest for you to believe? Talk to Him about this and ask Him for revelation in this area. Ask Him to show you this specific aspect of His heart throughout the coming week and then be looking for Him to show up and surprise you!*

LIFE TO THE FULL

I long for you to experience abundant,

overflowing life.

Zoe Life

"The thief comes only in order to steal and kill and destroy.
*I came that they may have and **enjoy life**, and have it in*
***abundance** (to the full, till it overflows)."*
John 10:10 Amplified Bible

Christ came so that we could enjoy abundant, overflowing life—"zoe" life. Zoe, the Greek word for eternal, abundant life, is found 36 times throughout the gospel of John and is defined as "blessed life, life that satisfies, life that is indwelt by God but not necessarily favored by circumstances."[1] This is the type of life that Christ meant for us to experience every single day: not a life filled with perfect circumstances, but a life that is utterly satisfying, completely blessed, and overflowing with the presence of God!

In his commentary, Barnes explains that the word abundance "denotes that which is not absolutely essential to life, but which is superadded to make life happy. They shall not merely have life—simple, bare existence—but they shall have all those superadded things which are needful to make that life eminently blessed and happy."[2] This is the extravagant God we serve, the generous God who gives us far more than we deserve or

---

[1] Spiros Zodhiates, *The Complete Word Study Dictionary New Testament* (Chattanooga: AMG Publishers)

[2] Albert Barnes' Notes on the Bible in Rick Meyers, *e-Sword*, Version 7.9.8, 2000-2008.

even need. God, the giver of zoe life in excessive, abundant, overflowing measures!

"Beloved, the whole reason I came to earth was so that you could experience true abundant life. This was worth leaving Heaven for. This was worth the cross. This was worth all the suffering and loneliness and grief I went through on earth. I didn't come to steal, kill, or destroy. That's what the enemy is about. Where he comes to steal, I come to give. Where he comes to kill, I come to bring life. Where he comes to destroy, I come to build and restore. Careful: he would like to deceive you about this, to convince you that I am out to steal your joy, kill your dreams, and destroy your life. But, Beloved, nothing could be farther from the truth. I have come to fill you with joy, breathe life into the dreams I've given you, and restore your life to a level of abundance you didn't know existed. This is what I am about. This is my heart for you. And I will never act in a way contrary to it.

Abundant life is when your heart and soul become truly alive throughout the day. It's not walking around with a heart that is numb or dead while pretending to be alive to those around you. It's life in which you are completely engaged in the day, living from your core, experiencing life, and living present to those around you and present to me. I want you to thrive, my girl! I don't want you just getting by, barely surviving the day. I want you to dance, smile, and *live* each day! Your quality of life should be so different from those who don't know me. They should look at you and the fullness in which you live and be amazed. This fullness isn't measured by **quantity**—doing more, serving more, cramming more "good" things into your day. It's measured by **quality**—the incredible quality of peace, joy, love, celebration, excitement, and power with which you live. Beloved, this is the abundant life I created you for."

* Breathing Exercise:

1. *Take a 10-minute break sometime today. If it's nice outside, take a walk or find a bench to sit on. Then breathe. Breathe deeply. Take three or four long, deep breaths and let go of the thoughts of the day so you can be present to God. He is with you and His heart for you in this moment and this day is zoe life. Allow your heart and soul to re-engage with Him and with the day. Find your heart—the place where He dwells. That's where you're to live from, not from your mind and a busy to-do list. Ask to see Him and to hear what's in His heart. Feel the sun on your face, notice the people around you and the miracles that they are, look up at His smile and allow it to spread to your face. Be still and know that He is God.*

Knowing Him

*"Now this is **eternal life**: that they may **know** you, the only true God, and Jesus Christ, whom you have sent."*
John 17:3

*"In him was **life**, and that life was the light of men."*
John 1:4

"Ultimately, Beloved, abundant life is knowing me. When you truly get to know me, everything about you will come alive. For in me is *life*! Everything I touch, breathe on, and speak over receives life. I am the source of all life, and as you step into my presence, you step into true life. You were created to know me, and the more you do, the more you will experience a quality of life that you didn't know existed. Abundant life comes when you begin to live in my presence, under my smile, holding my hand, and allowing my Spirit to take over your heart and body. It's the life you're going to experience for all eternity with me in Heaven. It's your destiny, Beloved.

Your destiny is an existence saturated with more joy, euphoria, beauty, delight, peace, and love than you can possibly imagine. I don't think you get this, because if you did, you wouldn't be worrying about all these little things in your life. There is a destiny ahead of you more glorious, breathtaking, and fulfilling than anything you can imagine, and it will be forever! This life on earth is a blink. These inconveniences of today—they are so small. Can you see how miniscule they are? Can you see how ridiculous it is to allow them to steal your joy and life? Paul understood this—that's why he was able to define imprisonment, starvation, and beatings as light and momentary troubles that were achieving for him an eternal glory that far outweighed them all, as he fixed his eyes not on what was seen, but on what was unseen.[1]

Beloved, abundant eternal life is your destiny, but it doesn't begin in Heaven—it starts *now*. Right now! Catch the vision and step into the abundance of eternity now. Set your heart on things above, not on earthly things.[2] Rise to a higher plane as you live life here in light of eternity. For in light of what's coming, how can you not have joy and peace in the midst of daily inconveniences, frustrating people, and long to-do lists?

Please don't miss it, my love. I went through so much for you to be able to experience life to the full, but it's possible to miss it if you're too caught up in yourself, the little inconveniences of the day, and the earthly circumstances around you. Rise up, Beloved; it's time to live on a Kingdom plane. I'm inviting you to join me here. I'm inviting you to a life of fullness. I'm inviting you to know me and know your destiny, and to step into life that is truly life."

* Breathing Exercises:

1. *Abundant life is found in knowing God, not in perfect circumstances. Any situation that allows you to get to know God better is a situation brimming with abundant life. Think of a difficult situation in your life and begin to tap into the well of abundant life found in this circumstance by seeking to know God more through it.*

---

[1] 2 Corinthians 4:17-18
[2] Colossians 3:2

Remember, He wants to reveal Himself to you. Don't miss the living water right before you!

2. *Take five minutes to set your heart and mind on things above instead of the earthly things around you.[3] Ask the Lord for a glimpse of what's happening in heaven right now. Ask for a vision of your destiny. Let your imagination go as you dream of your home and eternity there with Him. If you need some help, read Revelation 21—it paints an amazing picture for us!*

---

[3] Colossians 3:2

Christit, my life

*"When Christ, who is **your life**, appears, then you also will appear with him in glory." Colossians 3:4*

During the hardest eight months I've ever been through, God used the above verse to lead me into new truths about the abundant life He came to give us . . .

It was May of 2002, I had just completed my sophomore year of college at Azusa Pacific University, and I was ecstatic to be heading to Africa for the first time. I couldn't contain my excitement as I boarded a plane for Nairobi, Kenya with seven other team members from my school. Though I had no idea what my month in Kenya would hold, I knew the adventuresome God who was leading me there and couldn't wait for all that He had in store.

I wasn't disappointed. As I traveled throughout the rural villages, serving and living among the people there, my life was forever changed. My heart broke for the hopeless situations in which so many people seemed trapped, but I also fell in love. I fell in love with Kenya, the people, the culture, the land, and the heartbeat of Africa. As I boarded the plane to return to the States, I knew I was leaving behind a big piece of my heart and prayed that I would be allowed to return one day to find it. What I didn't know was that Kenya decided to leave something with me as well: a bug.

It wasn't until the trip home that I begin to notice the little sucker. My stomach began to feel pretty upset, but I wasn't too worried and figured whatever little bug was in there would soon find its way out of my body. But the little guy wasn't eager to leave. Even after multiple trips to the doctor and numerous doses of antibiotics, I still found myself getting worse by the day. After three weeks with no improvement, I had lost 18 pounds and an international disease specialist admitted me to the hospital to get some fluids in me and do some major testing. Somehow, the x-rays, CT scans, blood tests, and scopes down my throat into my stomach still failed to find the problem. Finally, they decided I must have some "unidentifiable virus" that is only found in Africa. So they sent me home saying that there was nothing they could do for me and they hoped my body would simply fight off the virus by itself. Wonderful—just wonderful.

As the summer months slowly droned on, my stomach began to calm down a bit, but nausea and overwhelming fatigue were still daily battles. Even talking took too much energy, and getting out of bed to walk to the bathroom was all the exercise I could manage. The best way I can describe it is that I always felt like I had just run a marathon and hadn't slept in five days. Family and friends cried out to God with me for healing, but it didn't come. God felt distant and aloof. As August rolled around, it became clear that returning to school that semester was out of the question. I remember days of weeping as my plans and dreams for the coming year were crushed and some of the things I had treasured most were stripped from me.

I soon became extremely depressed—something I had never experienced before. Though my family was an incredible blessing as they cared for and encouraged me day in and day out, I still found myself alone much of the day while they were at school and work. And I would weep. Most days I didn't even know why I was crying, but I'm sure the tears were flowing from some combination of my exhaustion, depression, loneliness, and hopelessness.

God, I cried out one day, *what are you doing? Your word says that you came to give us life and life to the full, but this feels like the farthest thing possible from life to the full. Where is the abundant life in this?*

His still small voice came, directing me to Colossians 3:4— *"When Christ, who is **your life**, appears, then you also will appear with him in glory."*

"Kierra, the secret to finding abundant life is making me your life: not just a part of your life, not even the most important part of your life; I want to be your entire life. Up until now, you have only allowed me to be a part of your life. School, ministry, work, and friends have become your main life. Now that they're stripped away, it feels like you have no life left. But, Beloved, you still have me, and in me is *life*. And since I will never leave you, you will have life in every circumstance, even right here alone in this bed. I am the source of true life—not all those other things you used to look to."

I knew He was right. I had made other things my life and I felt empty now that they were gone. I had grown up learning that God was all I truly needed, that He was the only one who could meet my every need and fulfill my every desire, that He was truly enough. But somehow the reality of my situation made all that sound like a joke. I could only cry and say, *God, I'm sorry. I long to make you my entire life, but I need your help to get there. I long to trust that you are truly enough, but it doesn't feel like you are right now, so please help me.*

It was a very slow process, but as I surrendered the things I had held so dearly, He was faithful to lead me into a daily, life-giving relationship with Him unlike anything I'd ever experienced. He truly became my *life*. It wasn't easy and it wasn't fun. I still found myself crying through most of my days, but I also found myself living in a new intimate and raw communion with God. And I found that He truly is enough! I began to learn through experience that abundant life isn't "happy" life; it's life to the full—but that means full of more things than happiness. It's life that is full of joy, peace, pain, hope, love, adventure, growth, mourning, laughter, tears, and most of all, **God**. It is, as I quoted before, "life indwelt by God, but not necessarily favored by circumstances."

My season of sickness ended with a miraculous healing on March 8, 2003. That day, a local Kenyan church prayed over me and later that evening eight friends laid hands on me begging for healing and deliverance. God responded, and the chains of the sickness broke. I woke up the next morning and felt like a completely different person. The nausea was gone, and I was able to walk and talk the entire day without an ounce of fatigue. It was **amazing**! Our God truly is a healer.

Could He have healed me the first week I prayed for it in June? Yes, but He had so much He wanted to do in my heart during those eight months of bed rest. And you know what? I'm so thankful. Even though they were the hardest eight months of my life, I wouldn't trade them for anything. His heart for us is abundant life, and for me that included eight months filled with sickness, tears, lessons, and intimacy with Him that changed my life forever. The lessons of those eight months provided a foundation that I will be able to stand on for the rest of my life. For I saw that no matter what else happens in life, God is enough! A life indwelt by Him is enough! And I know that if I continue to find my life in Him, I will experience abundant life in every situation that comes my way.

Yet, even six years later, I still wrestle with this. One of the deepest desires of my heart right now is to get married and serve overseas with my husband as we bring God's hope to people in need of His love. It is very easy for me to think that abundant life is found in that scenario. *Once I'm married and living overseas, then I'll really begin to enjoy abundant life.* But the truth is that abundant life is not found in marriage. And abundant life is not found in living overseas. Abundant life is found in God and God alone. And if I make marriage or ministry my life, I will be extremely disappointed. Those things can be stripped away—but not my God. He will never leave me, and if I make Him my life, then I have abundant life in any and every situation, even right now as a single girl living in the good ol' U.S.A.

Thank you, Lord! Thank you for the incredible gift of abundant life that you offer us every moment of every day. Thank you that this is your heart for us!

* Breathing Exercises:

1. *What things have you made your life? Where are you looking for life apart from Christ? Give those things to the Lord and repent of making something other than Him your 'god.' Invite Him to show you what it would look like for **Him** to become your life.*
2. *Spend five minutes meditating on Colossians 3:4—"When Christ, who is your life, appears, then you also will appear with him in glory." (To meditate simply means to reflect, contemplate, think deeply, pray, and listen to God.)*

FULLNESS OF JOY

I desire for my joy to be in you and

for your joy to be complete.

My Joy

*"And now I am coming to You [Father]; I say these things while I am still in the world, so that **My joy** may be made **full and complete and perfect in them** [that they may experience **My delight** fulfilled in them, that **My enjoyment** may be perfected in their own souls, that they may have **My gladness** within them, filling their hearts]." John 17:13 Amplified Bible*

*"If you keep My commandments [if you continue to obey My instructions], you will abide in My love and live on in it, just as I have obeyed My Father's commandments and live on in His love. I have told you these things, that **My joy and delight may be in you**, and that **your joy and gladness** may be of **full measure** and **complete** and **overflowing**."*
John 15:10-11 Amplified Bible

"Beloved, my heart longs for you to become a vessel flooded and overflowing with my joy. Not a momentary, fleeting joy of this world, but a deeper and richer joy—MY joy. My joy is completely separate from earthly joy and doesn't make sense in the natural realm. It is lasting, permanent, full, unexplainable, nonsensical, complete, true, and strong. But this joy does not come randomly. No, Beloved, it is *always* connected to *me* and to our relationship. My joy comes from my Spirit within you and is more delightful, more pleasing, more intoxicating, more healing, more transforming, more contagious, more radiant, more breath-taking, and more glorious than any joy this world can offer. This is the joy I want to fill you with. You've had moments where you've experienced this joy, but until now most of the joy you've experienced in life has been incomplete. It's been circumstantial, temporary, and easily overrun by the worries of the day. It hasn't been the strongest force in your life. Worry, stress, pressure, and seriousness have proven to be stronger forces for you. But *my* joy *is* stronger! And I want to deposit *my* joy in you! All you have to do is make room to receive it, allow me to fill you with it, and then learn to protect that joy, refusing to allow worry or problems to drive it out.

Seeing you filled with my joy brings a smile to my face and delight to my heart. I love to watch you bubble over with my joy! I love to see your smile and I love to hear your laughter—it brings joy to my own heart and we become connected by common joy. I love you, and I want to see you joyful, happy, smiling, and free! You bring me glory when you smile and laugh—you testify to my goodness and love when you allow my joy to fill you and spill out for those around you to see. It is true that I am most glorified in you when you are most satisfied in me."[1]

* Breathing Exercise:

1. *Do you believe this is God's heart for you? Do you believe it's possible for His joy to be in you and for your joy to be of full measure, complete, and overflowing? Bring all of your fears, doubts, pain, and baggage to Him. Lay them out honestly and allow Him to speak into them. Then spend some time soaking in the verses above. Ask the Lord to give you a 'heart revelation' of the truths found in them until you actually believe that these are His words and His heart for* **you**.

---

[1] John Piper, *Let the Nations be Glad* (Grand Rapids: Baker Academic, 2003), 31.

My Presence

*"You will show me the path of life; in Your presence is **fullness of joy**, at Your right hand there are pleasures forevermore." Psalm 16:11 Amplified Bible*

*"Blessed are those who have learned to acclaim you, who walk in the **light of your presence, O Lord**. They **rejoice** in your name all day long; they **exult** in your righteousness." Psalm 89:15-16*

"Beloved, I am inviting you to live your days in the light of my presence, under my smile, and sharing my joy. You have unrestricted access to my presence and you are invited to dwell here every moment of your life. The curtain in the temple has been torn, so the holy of holies is now available to any who desire to come.[1] It's up to you how far you want to come into my presence, and how long you want to remain.

I'm telling you, my love, that you will be amazed at the exorbitant joy, gladness, laughter, and rejoicing that is found in my presence. My child, I'm a belly-laugher with an irresistibly contagious laugh. I'm a smiler, and my eyes have a life-giving twinkle in them. Abundant, pure, and complete joy overflows out of every fiber of my being, and it will begin to seep into you as you spend time in my presence. Yes, I also feel the pain of my hurting children, and I hurt with them, but pain has no power to diminish my joy. I am able to simultaneously

---

[1] Matthew 27:51

25

grieve with you while maintaining my joyful essence. Joy is an indestructible part of my nature and dwelling place—one of the fruits and permanent qualities of my Spirit—and one of my favorite things to do is to share my joy with my children. The joy, peace, and love found in my presence are completely infectious, and you will catch them when you see and experience me. You'll never want to leave my presence once you experience my all-consuming joy.

Beloved, in my presence there is no pressure, no anxiety, no hurry, and no fear. There is only divine peace, joy, love, hope and beauty. I'm inviting you to dwell with me in this place, this state of mind and heart, instead of dwelling in the hurried, anxious, stress-filled place you live most days. I know that you long to live in the contagious joy of my presence, to hear my laughter and to join me in it. I know you are hungry to see the twinkle in my eyes, but the demands of the day always seem to press in and worry you, causing you to think that living every moment aware of my presence is impossible.

Well, I'm telling you today that it's very possible—it's actually the reality I created you to live in. So I invite you to come, Beloved. Come start your day in my presence. Seek my face in the morning with all your heart. You must make time for this—for you can't remain with me throughout the day if you never enter my presence in the first place. Set your heart and mind on things above, not on earthly things.[2] Ask for my perspective on your day as it begins, and then continue to ask as we walk together throughout the day. Every time you encounter a problem or a need, turn your heart to me and remember I am present. If there comes a moment when you realize you are completely absorbed in the earthly cares around you, take a few minutes to quiet your heart and center yourself back into the truth that

---

[2] Colossians 3:1-2

I am right there with you. Tune your soul to what's going on in my throne room as you fix your eyes not on what is seen but on what is unseen.[3] You can allow the circumstances around you to be your focus, or you can maintain eye contact with me throughout the day, staying continually aware of my joy-filled presence as we walk together. Beloved, we're partners in life, and you are never alone. Remembering this again and again is what abiding is all about, and it is worth the time it takes. You bring me ever-increasing glory as you walk in the light of my presence, rejoicing and exulting in me throughout the day. This glorifies me far more than when you are simply "efficient", accomplishing a lot of tasks in my name without my life and power flowing through you. Flesh gives birth to flesh, but the Spirit gives birth to spirit.[4] Truly, apart from me you can do nothing of eternal value, so there's no point in continuing throughout your day disconnected from me. Just stop; realign your heart, and we can go on together from there.

Beloved, may I tell you a secret? You'll be surprised by what you discover as you stay conscious of me throughout your daily routines. I am very fun and much less serious than you perceive me to be! Listen for my jokes and my laughter. Yes, I know there is pain all around you, but remember my joy can coexist with pain. I know how to ache and laugh; I see the end from the beginning. I know what I'm doing, what I'm teaching those around you, and you can trust me. You are my child and I'd love to have fun with you. I want to show you my sense of humor. There's so much more to my character and heart than you know—so many fun surprises that you'll discover during our time together throughout your day.

---

[3] 2 Corinthians 4:18
[4] John 3:6

I want to help you with this, and I will give you the grace for this walk. I am committed to teaching you the practice of abiding in my presence. Make the pursuit of my presence the one thing you seek[5] and I will faithfully lead you into a life-giving experience with me. Put forth the energy and time to dwell in my presence, and I will give you deeper and deeper revelations. From there, my everlasting joy will begin to wash over you and radiate out onto all those around you. Are you ready? Do you want this close connection with me? I have given you my invitation; now it's up to you to respond."

* Breathing Exercises:

1. *Commit to beginning each day this week in the Lord's presence. Meditate on Psalms 27:4 and 89:15-16. Then seek to remain conscious of His presence for the rest of the day. Do a heart-check every hour to see where your focus is. Are you more aware of the joy-filled presence of the Lord, or of the burdens around you? If your heart has wandered off course, take the time to center it back onto the ever-present, all-powerful, joyful God who **is** with you!*

    "One thing I ask of the Lord, this is what I seek: that I may dwell in the house of the Lord all the days of my life, to gaze upon the beauty of the Lord and to seek him in his temple." Psalm 27:4

    *"Blessed are those who have learned to acclaim you, who walk in the **light of your presence, O Lord**. They **rejoice** in your name all day long; they **exult** in your righteousness." Psalm 89:15-16*

---

[5] Psalm 27:4

2. *Take some time to go to a park or another area where children will be present. Watch and enjoy them. Children are made in God's image and give us delightful glimpses into His playfulness, humor, and joy. Watch them play and listen for God's laughter as He plays with them and enjoys them. If you've been plagued with the serious bug lately, be brave and join their fun! Take some time to play with the Lord—be it finger-painting, going on the swings, running after the ice-cream man, playing a board game, reading a goofy children's book, or watching a funny movie. Get creative and allow the Lord to take you on a fun date!*

Remain and Obey

*"**As the Father has loved me, so have I loved you**. Now **remain in my love**. If you obey my commands, you will **remain in my love**, just as I have obeyed my Father's commands and **remain in his love**. I have told you this so that **my joy may be in you** and that **your joy may be complete**." John 15:9-11*

"Beloved, do you realize that I love you with the same intensity, passion, and depth that the Father loves me? Oh, how I long for you to grasp this. I love you with an all-consuming love. Receiving a revelation of the depths of my love for you is pivotal. Your overflowing joy hinges on this and I am committed to giving you this revelation. I'm actually much more committed to giving it to you than you are to receiving or even seeking it. Ask me for understanding, my child, and prepare your heart to receive my love.

When I share a part of my heart with you or an aspect of my love, I want you to remain in it, sit with it, dwell in it, meditate on it, and abide in it. You're always so quick to move on to the next thing: the next book you want to read or the next activity you want to do. But the quality, caliber, and depth of the truths I want to reveal to you require some soaking time—actually, a lot of soaking time—otherwise they end up going in one ear and out the other, missing your heart altogether. Remain in my love, my child; sit with the truths in the scriptures and in this book. As you allow them to soak-in until you feel saturated, you will discover that indescribable joy is waiting just around the corner!

Beloved, another part of remaining in my love and experiencing my overflowing joy involves listening to and obeying my instructions to you for this season of life. Every instruction I give you is for your joy and wholeness—spoken to teach you how to remain in my life-giving love. I don't give you commands to add more things to your "to-do" list. I don't even like "to-do" lists. They take you away from me and steal the life, joy, and relationship I'm offering you. They make you feel like you are in control of your day, and they weigh you down. I want to partner with you in a way that does not make you feel heavy and encumbered. My commands are meant to free you so that you might experience the joy you were created for. My commands are meant to give you life. And Kierra, these are my instructions to you for this season of life:

1. Bask in me and my love
2. Continue to get to know my heart for you
3. Dive into my word
4. Allow yourself to rest on the Sabbath so you can be still and know that I am God

As you spend time in my throne room responding to my invitation to intimacy, you will learn that anything else I ask of you in life is also going to be for your joy. Your reluctance to obey what I ask only postpones the promises that I have for you. So listen daily for my instructions, Beloved, and obey them. Once you do and you learn to remain in my powerful love, you won't be able to stop overflowing with my joy—the joy that comes from knowing you are completely and unconditionally loved."

* Breathing Exercises:

1. *Spend ten minutes soaking in Christ's words in John 15:9, practicing the discipline of abiding. Remain in the truths of this scripture and allow them to remain in you.*

Stay here. Remain in His love and dwell in His words. Let these truths soak into every fiber of your heart and mind.

"As the Father has loved me, so have I loved you. Now remain in my love." John 15:9

2. *Ask the Lord if He has any specific instructions for you during this season of your life. He is eager to share His heart with you. So ask, listen, and then record what you hear. The commands in the Bible are always true for you, and you need to continually obey them, but God may also have specific instructions at this time just for you. Listen to them, record them, and then step into full obedience—it is these commands that will lead you down the path toward the fullness of joy He created you for.*

Ask Me!

*"I tell you the truth, my Father will give you whatever you ask in my name. Until now you have not asked for anything in my name. Ask and you will receive, and **your joy will be complete.**" John 16:23-24*

"Beloved, I want you to experience the fullness of joy that comes from asking and receiving from me. I ***want*** you to come to me and ask for the desires of your heart, and I ***want*** you to experience the joy of receiving them from me. I ***want*** to pour out love gifts on you and I ***want*** them to bring you joy. I ***want*** to bless you.

I'm inviting you to come boldly to my throne room to be with me. Come share your heart with me: your desires, your worries, and your longings. Ask for what you want and need. It's ok to ask me—in fact, I'm inviting you to. It doesn't mean you're selfish or self-consumed. It simply means that you've caught a vision of my generous heart toward you and you want to tap into it. It means you're beginning to understand how much I love you and how I long to work on your behalf and respond to your requests. It means you're stepping into the incredible intimacy I desire for us to share—an intimacy in which we freely share the desires of our hearts with one another. I love it when you come to ***me*** with your needs. So often I'm the last person people come to with their burdens, but I long to be the first! I long for my children to trust my heart and power enough to confidently run to me with every concern and desire. I am a *good* Father and there are so many good gifts I want to pour out on you if only you will ask!

And then after asking, Beloved, learn to receive the gifts that I generously pour out in response to your requests. Right now, you don't know how to receive and treasure my gifts to you. I'm giving you so many, but you're not really enjoying them. I want to give you grace to receive and enjoy them, as well as to enjoy me and my goodness in the process. So often you feel guilty for enjoying my gifts to you while others seem to be lacking them. That's like one of your married friends feeling guilty for enjoying her husband while you're still single. I've given each of you different gifts, and it brings me glory when you praise me for the gifts I've given *you* and when you enjoy them and experience my love for you through them.

The expression of my love for you is found in far more than the intangible thoughts you have as you sit quietly with me. I'm constantly pouring my love out to you in the form of little gifts and surprises, but you must be present to notice that these gifts are coming from my hand. My gifts come in a variety of forms: a kind word from a friend, a beautiful sunset, a juicy nectarine, some free time, an opportunity to pray with someone. But the evil one tries to distract you from recognizing these gifts and to keep you so busy that you don't even see, much less enjoy them. Oh, how I long for you to slow down, notice, and **enjoy** me, my love, my joy, my surprises, and my laughter. This is worship! This pleases me! This makes you come alive and brings me glory. Beloved, I didn't create you to always be serious and responsible; I also created you to laugh, to skip, to dance, and to enjoy my creation and gifts throughout the day. You're missing so much when you rush past the sweetness of life and overlook my gifts for you. Learn to taste and see and enjoy! I want to teach you the art of pure enjoyment, of celebration, of holy leisure! Trust me and let me teach you. Ask and you will *receive* and your joy will be complete!"[1]

* Breathing Exercises:

1. *Carve out some time in your day to respond to God's invitation to ask. Quiet your mind and the outside noise and come before your caring Father for a heart-to-heart talk. Share the desires of your heart with Him and ask for them. Ask in faith, trusting that He* **loves** *to fulfill your deepest desires. Listen to His heart as well and allow Him to share the desires of His heart with you. Let this be an intimate time of sharing your hearts with one another. Then start looking for His answers throughout the coming weeks. He loves to say "Yes" to you and wants you to fully enjoy the expression of His "Yes."*

2. *Be alert to God's extravagant gifts this day. Ask Him to open your eyes to the love gifts all around you, and then allow yourself to* **enjoy** *them! Determine to fully enjoy every love gift that your doting Father pours out on you today. You may have to slow down a bit, you might look a little silly, but you will definitely delight the heart of your Father as you revel in His goodness and love!*

---

[1] John 16:24

An Anointing of Joy

"The Spirit of the Sovereign Lord is on me, because the Lord
*has anointed me to . . . bestow on them the **oil of gladness***
*instead of mourning, and a **garment of praise** instead of a*
spirit of despair." Isaiah 61:1,3

"Therefore God, your God, has set you above your
*companions by **anointing you with the oil of joy.***"
Psalm 45:7b

"You prepare a table before me in the presence of my enemies.
*You **anoint my head with oil**; my cup overflows."*
Psalm 23:5

Joy is a gift that God loves to anoint us with. It's not something
we always have to work for—it is simply a gift of His Spirit
that He loves to pour out on us. He's committed to our joy
and delights to anoint us with His life-giving oil of gladness.
When the Bible was written, oil was used on occasions of
festivity and celebration but abstained from in times of public
calamity or grief. When people began to anoint their heads with
oil, you knew it was party time! The oil represented joy and
was an outward expression of the person's inward celebration
and rejoicing. It indicated divine favor and prosperity. Much
as we prepare ourselves for celebrations today by dressing up,
applying make-up, and looking our best, the ancient festival
customs included anointing the head with oil.1

---

[1] Albert Barnes, *e-Sword*

The Israelites would have read the above scriptures with a clear understanding of this symbolism of oil. It's we who miss the significance today. God longs to anoint our heads with the oil of His joy and lead us into a life of divine celebration and rejoicing! The year of the Lord's favor is here and it's time to celebrate![2] He is all about celebration and loves to pour out His favor and joy in overflowing portions into our lives. I love the literal interpretation of Psalm 23:5 where David says, "You anoint my head with oil." In the Hebrew, this literally means "makest fat", and translates, "Thou dost pour oil on my head so abundantly that it seems to be made fat with it."[3] Isn't that awesome? This isn't just a little bit of oil that God pours on him—it's so much oil that David feels fat with it. Now that's a lot of oil! When God anoints us with his joy, this is the picture of the abundance he wants to pour out onto us.

When we anoint people with oil in churches today, we usually dab a few drops on their forehead. But in ancient times, they would saturate the 'anointed one' with oil. Psalm 133:2 talks about the oil running down Aaron's beard onto his clothes. This was messy business! God still bestows this type of anointing today. In John 3:34, it says that God gives the Spirit "without limit". He longs to fill us with His Spirit in limitless, overflowing measures. And one of the fruits of this Spirit is **joy**! So when we get the Spirit without limit, we also receive joy without limit. It's time to celebrate, friends! The time of singing and celebration has come.

"Beloved, I really do want to bestow on you the oil of gladness. I long to fill you with extravagant amounts of joy. I want to anoint your head with the oil of my joy until you are completely fat with it. I want to give you my Spirit without limit. Just come

---

[2] Isaiah 61:2
[3] Albert Barnes, *e-Sword*

stand under me and ask. Ask for the oil of my joy and I'll give it. Ask for my Spirit and I'll give it. I love to give them—there's nothing I delight to do more. So often you come to me, allow me to put a drop of oil on your forehead, and then you race off to your next activity. You settle for so little, ask for so little, and expect so little.

But Beloved, I delight to anoint you with extravagant, limitless joy. I am inviting you into a perpetual lifestyle of celebration—continuous no matter what circumstances you find yourself in. Celebrate and rejoice in me, my presence, my unconditional love, my power, my heart, my gifts, my hope, and the daily victories I give you. I don't promise you a pain-free life, but I do promise to lead you into an experience of *my joy* that transcends circumstances, if you'll only let me teach you and fill you with it. I am for you, my love, and I am for your joy. I long for you to become a radiant vessel, anointed and overflowing with my joy."

* Breathing Exercises:

1. *Ask the Lord for a fresh anointing of His joy! Spend time in His presence and allow yourself to simply receive from Him. Ask Him to fill you with overflowing measures of His Spirit and joy.*
2. *Choose to celebrate today. No matter what situation you find yourself in, there is much to celebrate! God is on His throne, advancing His Kingdom and preparing to come back for **you**. You have an eternity in heaven awaiting you, the unconditional love and acceptance of your Heavenly Father, the deep companionship of the One who promises to never leave or forsake you, and the King of the universe working all things together for your*

good!⁴ Now those are some great reasons to celebrate. Choose to celebrate them today, along with the gift of life, salvation, redemption, and the relationships God's given you. May your example invite others to join the celebration with you!

Final Words from the Father

"Beloved, I want to finish here by clarifying that I don't expect you to be permanently joyful and happy. When a friend has just been killed in a car accident, or a child is diagnosed with leukemia, or a spouse has cheated on his wife and is filing for divorce, it's good to grieve, be heartbroken, and feel the deep pain. There are seasons to grieve, mourn, and hurt, and I want you to feel and walk through those emotions with me. I'm not instructing you to just put on a happy face and be completely joyful in every situation. What I *do* want to communicate is that my heart is committed to filling you with my unconquerable joy. Sometimes trials and pain are necessary for your joy as I purify you and make you whole and complete. That's not the reason for all pain—there is definitely an adversary who is seeking to steal, kill, and destroy your joy—and you live in a fallen world where people have the free will to cause one another pain. But despite all of this, my heart longs to fill you with my joy and for your joy to be complete! This is what I long for you to hear and believe."

---

⁴ John 14:1-4, Psalm 13:5, Psalm 118:1, Deuteronomy 31:8, Romans 8:28

FULL DELIGHT

I delight in and am delighted by you.

Selah

Have you ever noticed the word 'Selah' that seems to randomly appear after certain stanzas in the Psalms? Ever wondered what it means or why it's there? I have. So I looked it up one day and learned that it means "pause and calmly consider that." Interesting, huh? Knowing our tendency to skim over words and truth, the writers inserted a literal pause to make us slow down and soak in the depth and meaning of what was just said. They inserted 'speed bumps' to keep us from racing ahead too quickly and missing the richness of the message. I love it—I personally need that instruction included in the text. My fast-paced, task-oriented mind loves to quickly consume chapters of the Bible much like I consume my oatmeal in the morning. I read quickly in an effort to feel good about what I have accomplished and then efficiently move on to the next activity in my schedule. I'm not naturally prone to pause and calmly consider a particular passage. Consequently, I end up missing out on many of God's deep treasures that are waiting to be discovered.

For this reason, I'm learning to treasure each Selah dispersed throughout Scripture. I'm learning to heed these speed bumps so that I don't miss the treasures to which they point. Today, I want to insert my own Selah's as God shares His heart through Scripture. You may have read these scriptures many times in the past, but today I invite you to listen to His words at a deeper level—to pause and calmly consider what He is trying to communicate to you. The truths contained in these statements are life-changing. As you read His words, listen carefully to

His heart. Ask Him to reveal to you what He means in each sentence or thought. Ask for a heart revelation of these truths. He longs for you to understand the depths of His delight and pleasure in you.

*"The Lord your God is with you, he is mighty to save. He will take **great delight** in you, he will quiet you with his love, he will **rejoice over you** with singing." Zephaniah 3:17*

Selah

*"You have **stolen my heart**, my sister, my bride; you have stolen my heart with one glance of your eyes, with one jewel of your necklace. **How delightful is your love**, my sister, my bride! How much more **pleasing is your love** than wine, and the fragrance of your perfume than any spice! Your lips drop sweetness as the honeycomb, my bride; milk and honey are under your tongue. The fragrance of your garments is like that of Lebanon." Song of Songs 4:9-11*

Selah

*"How beautiful you are and how **pleasing**, O love, with **your delights**!" Song of Songs 7:6*

Selah

*"I belong to my lover, and his **desire is for me**." Song of Songs 7:10*

Selah

*"**His pleasure** is not in the strength of the horse, nor his delight in the legs of a man; the Lord **delights** in those who fear him, who put their hope in his unfailing love." Psalm 147:10-11*

Selah

"Let Israel rejoice in their Maker; let the people of Zion be glad in their King. Let them praise his name with dancing and make

*music to him with tambourine and harp. For the **Lord takes
delight in his people**; he crowns the humble with salvation.
Let the saints rejoice in this honor and sing for joy on their beds."
Psalm 149:2-3*

Selah

*"No longer will they call you Deserted, or name your land
Desolate. But you will be called Hephzibah (my delight is in her),
and your land Beulah (married); for the Lord will **take delight
in you**, and your land will be married . . . As a bridegroom
rejoices over his bride, so will your God **rejoice over you**."
Isaiah 62:4,5b*

Selah

*"And you will be called **Sought After**, the City No Longer
Deserted." Isaiah 62:12b*

Selah

* Breathing Exercises:

1. *Which of these scriptures had the most impact on you?
   Write it on an index card that you can carry with you
   the rest of the day. Read it every half hour and ask the
   Lord to drive that truth deeper and deeper into your
   heart.*
2. *Think of a person for whom you would like to better
   understand God's heart. It may be a family member,
   your spouse, a friend who doesn't know Him yet, or
   someone who is frustrating and difficult to be around.
   Slowly read through these scriptures again, but this time
   read them as God sharing His heart for that person. As
   you read, ask God to overwhelm you and fill you with
   His heart for that child of His. If one scripture stands out
   to you or if the Lord gives you specific insight into His*

heart for that person, share it with him or her! Secretly, everyone would love to hear an encouraging message about God's heart for them. There's no telling what God may do through your boldness to share that message.

The Father's Delight

*"You have **stolen my heart**, my sister, my bride; you have
stolen my heart with one glance of your eyes, with one jewel
of your necklace. **How delightful is your love**, my sister, my
bride! How much more **pleasing is your love** than wine!"*
Song of Songs 4:9-10a

*"The Lord your God is with you, he is mighty to save. He will
take **great delight** in you, he will quiet you with his love, he
will **rejoice over you** with singing." Zephaniah 3:17*

*"I belong to my lover, and his **desire is for me**."*
Song of Songs 7:10

*Oh, Lord, as I reflect on these verses, I don't understand how
I could have stolen your heart and how you could take such
delight in me. It seems crazy! I should be delighting in **you**.
You are the one who is worth delighting in and should steal my
heart. Yet, you continue to delight in me, even though I am so
wrapped up in myself that I completely forget about you many
days. I'm a harlot, Lord; I confess my love to you in the morning
and then go off with my other lovers throughout the day. How
is it that you continue to delight and take great pleasure in me?
Help me understand.*

"Beloved, you **have** stolen my heart and I **do** take great delight
in you. You are worthy of the depths of my delight and love
because you are my child and I deem you worthy—not because
of your actions or your reciprocation of my love. I created you

to love you, and I will continue loving you and delighting in you throughout all eternity. My child, I enjoy you! You make me smile. You make me smile simply by being you. My eyes twinkle when they look at you. They twinkle and dance and laugh—you'll see it if you look into them.

Do you want to know how much I delight in you? You put a song in my heart. I rejoice over you with singing![1] I really do. You make me want to sing. The delights of your love ignite singing in my throne room. You know when someone has captured your heart and you just find yourself humming? That's how I feel. And it's all because of you—your eyes, your nose, your laugh, your gentleness, your depth, your heart, everything about your personality—I'm totally tickled by you and captured by you. Not because of anything you do, but because of whom I made you to be—because you're my child. My heart overflows with joy because of you and I can't keep it in—I have to express it. The expression of the joy you bring me is rejoicing.

My desire is for *you*. I desire you and your heart and your love so deeply. I desire intimacy with you. I desire your love, affection, and faithfulness. I desire unity with you. I desire your trust and loyalty. I long for you to love me with all that you are and to delight in me the way I delight in you. I long for your heart to be captured by me. I don't need this in order to be complete or fulfilled. In fact, your lack of reciprocation never changes my love for you. My love and delight are unconditional whether they are returned or not; but, oh, I would love for the thought of me to put a smile on your face the way you put a smile on mine. I want my love to put a song in your heart. I want you to hum throughout the day because of me. I would love for your eyes to twinkle and dance when you look at me. I would love for you to delight in me the way I delight in you—for who

---

[1] Zephaniah 3:17

I am, not what I do. It's not hard—for I am overflowing with every delightful quality imaginable and unimaginable.

Enjoy and rest in my pleasure over you, Beloved. You are loved exactly as you are; no more striving to be someone you aren't. You are completely delightful as you are—as I made you. Smile today, for I am smiling over you. I am delighting over you. Soak up this favor and love. Enter my joy and laughter this day—drink of these rivers of delight with me."

* Breathing Exercises:

1. *Set aside 10 minutes to delight in the Lord and enjoy His delight over you. Ask to see the smile on His face and the twinkle in His eye that shines when He looks at you. Ask Him why He is smiling. Write down anything He shares with you. Then pick one of your favorite qualities about Him and share it with Him. Worship Him for it; delight in who He is.*
2. *As you go about your day, ask the Lord to give you a heart revelation of how much He delights in each person with whom you come into contact. Ask to see the way He smiles over them and for His smile from heaven to spread to your own face. Delight with the Lord in those around you. Be a vessel through which they can experience His delight.*

FULLY GOOD

I will never withhold any good thing from you.

A Good Father

*"Which of you, if his son asks for bread, will give him a stone? Or if he asks for a fish, will give him a snake? If you, then, though you are evil, know how to give good gifts to your children, **how much more will your Father in heaven give good gifts** to those who ask him!" Matthew 7:9-11*

*"Therefore I tell you, do not worry about your life, what you will eat or drink; or about your body, what you will wear . . . Look at the birds of the air; they do not sow or reap or store away in barns, and yet your heavenly Father feeds them. Are you not **much more valuable** than they? Who of you by worrying can add a single hour to his life?" Matthew 6:25-27*

"Beloved, I am a *good* father and I find such delight in being a father! I am the father who is *always* there for you, looking out for your best, providing exactly what you need, giving good gifts, and overflowing with oceans of love for you. I love being your dad!

I have adopted you as my daughter and you are worth more to me than you can ever imagine. You are far more valuable than the birds of the air, though even they have enough value to me that I care for them each day of their lives. The needs of every sparrow, every insect, every animal, and every plant are ever before me and I care about them. I value them enough to take care of them and provide for their needs. Yet Beloved, their worth pales in comparison to the worth *you* have to me. It's like the difference for a mother between her garden and her son.

She cares for the garden and tends to it, but it doesn't begin to compare to the worth of her child and the love she pours out to care for *him*. Beloved, this is how I feel about you. You mean more to me than you will ever be able to comprehend, and I will care for you with loving kindness every day of your life.

Once you begin to get a revelation of your insurmountable worth to me, it will be difficult to worry about your life. Because worrying is foolishness in light of your immeasurable value to me as my daughter and the power and riches I possess to intervene on your behalf. Just as an earthly dad finds joy in providing for the needs of his children, so I find deep joy in providing for you. And Beloved, I not only have everything you need today, I also have a plan and provision for tomorrow. You worry about the future so much and how you will provide for yourself, but Beloved, I will provide for you. Trust me my girl; I care about your needs more than you realize. I'm not worried about how I will provide for you in the future. I own all the riches in the world, as well as riches in heaven that you can't begin to imagine. I'm excited to surprise you and bless you with my provision.

When you worry about finances, it's like the daughter of a zillionaire worrying about money and where her provision is going to come from. Silly girl, I've got you covered. That doesn't mean I'm going to hand you everything on a silver platter your whole life, but it does mean you never need to worry. I won't leave you hanging. Ever. Yes, I'll teach you to work and to save and to steward finances well, but I don't teach you these lessons for you to become your own provider. I will always be your provider, but I will teach you to steward well all that I provide. You get this mixed up. When I teach you about saving and responsibility, you start thinking that that I'm passing on the role of provider to you. But that's a job I plan to hold on to. So Beloved, let go of the self-reliant, provider role that you've been trying to fill. It doesn't suit you well. It makes you anxious, serious, and stressed-out. I'm inviting you to step into your identity as a daughter. I love who you are when you fully embrace this identity—you become joyful, confident, and free! I've adopted you, now trust me to provide for you. I will meet all your needs. You are a deeply loved and cherished daughter of mine and you have no reason to worry about your future or provision.

Instead of worrying, start seeking my Kingdom! Enter into the grandness of the story around you. I am the King of Kings and am spreading my Kingdom of love, joy, and peace across the entire world. I am defeating darkness and rescuing a lost and hurting human race. Come enter this story and join me in my mission! It's such a greater adventure than living in your small little story worrying about food, clothes, shelter, etc. Seek me, seek the advance of my Kingdom, and enter the most exciting adventure of all time—I will take care of your needs!"

* Breathing Exercises:

1. *Which identity do you most embrace and live in each day: a self-reliant provider, or a son/daughter of the King of Kings? If you have trouble identifying with the son/daughter reality, what might be some of the reasons? Ask the Lord to give you a greater revelation of who He is as your Father and who you are as His child. How can that truth affect the way you live your days?*

2. *If you find yourself worrying often, it probably means that you don't yet understand your incredible value to God. If you need revelation here, ask Him to speak to you about your value to Him. Listen and write down any words that you hear His Spirit speaking to you. Then as you walk about your day, notice the birds, the squirrels, and the insects. God faithfully takes care of*

these creatures and He will faithfully take care of you who are much more valuable than they. Let the birds chirping outside remind you of the faithful provision of God and your infinite value to Him.

From the Beginning

"For the Lord God is a Sun and a Shield; the Lord bestows [present] grace and favor and [future] glory (honor, splendor, and heavenly bliss)! **No good thing will He withhold from those who walk uprightly.** *O Lord of hosts, blessed (happy, fortunate, to be envied) is the man who trusts in You [leaning and believing on You, committing all and confidently looking to You, and that without fear or misgiving]!"*
Psalm 84:11-12 Amplified Bible.

"The lions may grow weak and hungry, but those who seek the Lord **lack no good thing**.*" Psalm 34:10*

"Beloved, my heart towards you overflows with abundant goodness, and I want to bestow on you good gifts beyond your imagination. I *love* to bless my children! This is my heart for you. I find so much delight in showering you with good gifts. I desire for you to live the fullest, most abundant life possible on earth. I am not a stingy God, nor a God who withholds to keep you miserable and poor. If I withhold something from you, you can trust that it's not good for you: it's not beneficial, life-giving, the right timing, or something that will draw you closer to me. I am *for* you and I don't want things in your life that pull you down, distract you, or keep you from any of the amazing things I have in store for you.

Think back on the garden at the creation of the world; imagine it for a moment. I created it exactly as I wanted it. I created a whole garden for Adam to enjoy and delight in. My entire creation was very good and I gave it fully to him. I gave him every seed-bearing plant and every fruitful tree for food.[1] And it was delicious, healthy, life-giving food! My heart delighted to pour out my abundant goodness on him.

But then I saw that it was ***not good*** for Adam to be alone, so I brought him Eve. I wanted a ***good*** helper for him and after going through all the beasts that I had created, Adam and I knew that none of them would be enough. I am not a God who settles for something that's just "ok" or "will have to do." I wanted the best partner possible for him! So I made her specifically for him and brought her to him as a perfect love gift from my heart.[2] (When I give a gift to my child, it is always ***good***. I refuse to settle for anything less for my children. Sometimes they choose to settle for less than my best, but that is their choice. When it is in my hands, I will never settle for second best for them—that's just not in my nature or character).

I gave Adam and Eve an abundance of good gifts to enjoy, but I commanded them not to eat from the tree of the knowledge of good and evil because I knew it was not good for them.[3] I knew the destruction, death, and pain that eating of it would cause and the separation from me and each other it would bring. I knew they couldn't correctly handle that knowledge and the horrible eternal implications that would follow.

Unfortunately, they did not trust my heart towards them or obey my command. They judged what was good for them by their

---

[1] Genesis 1:1-31
[2] Genesis 2:18-25
[3] Genesis 2:16-17

own eyes and understanding, not by my words to them. They didn't trust that I was a God who would withhold no good thing from them. Instead, they trusted the serpent who convinced them that I was withholding something good because I felt threatened by their ability to become like me if they ate of the fruit. And so when they saw that the fruit was *"good for food and pleasing to the eye, and also desirable for gaining wisdom,"* they ate.[4] All of humankind is still experiencing the horrific consequences. And today, many of my children still distrust my good heart for them and continue to eat of the "fruit" that I withhold.

Beloved, I am inviting you to a different path; the path of trust. Will you trust my good heart? Don't let the enemy deceive you. My heart wants the best for you, and will never withhold any good thing from you. Walk in trust and enter the depths of the joys and gifts I want to offer you. The path I set before you lacks no good thing. If you choose other paths, you will miss out on some of my good gifts, but on those days, if you seek my direction I will lead you back to the path of life, where you will never miss out on an ounce of my goodness."

* Breathing Exercise:

1. *What "good" thing do you believe the Lord is withholding from you right now? How is the enemy trying to deceive you about God's intentions towards you? Enter a conversation with the Lord about this. If you need to confess areas of mistrust or misjudgment of His character, do it. If you need help seeing the truth amidst the lies that the enemy is feeding you, ask God to show you the truth. Use Psalm 84:11-12 as a weapon against the attacks of the enemy. Don't give in to his lies so easily—fight back!*

---

[4] Genesis 3:6

*Fight hard and send him running! Submit to God, resist the devil, and he **will** flee from you.[5]*

"For the Lord God is a sun and shield; the Lord bestows favor and honor; no good thing does he withhold from those whose walk is blameless. O Lord Almighty, blessed is the man who trusts in you." Psalm 84:11-12

---

[5] James 4:7

Times of Withholding

*Lord, I hear you promise that you withhold no good things from your children, but it doesn't seem like that's always true. What about the times when you **have** withheld your blessings from your people?*

"Yes, Beloved, there are times when I withhold my blessings from my people, but even this is for their *good*. Two of the most common reasons I withhold blessings at certain times are: for the wholeness of my people, and for the sake of my Kingdom. Let me explain . . .

For Their Wholeness

Sometimes I withhold what *seem* to be good things from my children for their wholeness and their best. I withheld the Promised Land from the Israelites for a long season in the desert because they needed to know me as their provider and Almighty God before they entered it. Had I not, they would have lacked the strength and confidence in me to take the land and remain in it. They needed to know me first—my character and my heart for them—in order to conquer and enjoy the land. I wanted them to take full, lasting possession of it, so I had to withhold it while I prepared and matured them.

Still, there was a generation who missed out on the Promised Land all together. They never learned to trust me—despite my miracles and constant provision during their time in the wilderness. They still chose to rely on what they could see instead of me. No matter how many times I provided water from a rock and manna from heaven, they continued to complain and grumble, getting caught up in the circumstances around them instead of my promises and character.[1] They never fully trusted my heart for them. When I finally brought them to the border of the Promised Land, they lacked the faith to enter. I would have given it to them; I was ready and excited. Yes, there were giants in the land, but I was ready to powerfully defeat those giants and lead the Israelites victoriously into the land. But they didn't trust my leadership or my strength to defeat their enemies. Instead, they accused me of bringing them on the entire journey through the wilderness only to watch them die at the hands of these giants. The land was theirs for the taking, but it could only be taken by faith and trust in me. So only Joshua and Caleb from that generation were able to enter. The rest died without receiving my fullness for them. It broke my heart, but the gift could only be received through faith.[2]

Oh Beloved, this journey of learning to trust my heart towards you is so crucial. For it is only through this deep trust and faith in me that you will be able to receive the incredible gifts I want to bestow on you. Learn from the Israelites. Get to know my character so that when I invite you to take possession of *your* Promised Lands, you will be able to follow me in faith and live in the blessing and fullness for which I created you!

As you follow me, Beloved, I promise to withhold no good thing from you. But you need to understand that sometimes

---

[1] Exodus 16:1-17:7
[2] Numbers 13:26-14:30

what's *good* for you isn't exactly fun or enjoyable. Sometimes what's good for you is a lesson in patience, or participation in the fellowship of my suffering and experiencing me as the Great Comforter, or enduring through a trial that teaches you perseverance and develops your character.[3] Sometimes what's best for you is time in my refining fire that perfects you, cleanses you, and shapes you into my image. My child, I love you too much to withhold the hard times from you. I love you far too much to shelter you from them, because many of them will lead you to a deeper maturity, peace, and joy than you could ever gain from an "easy" life. Truly my Beloved, *no* good thing will I withhold from you.

For the Sake of the Kingdom

Beloved, there are other times when I withhold things for the sake of my name and glory. But my child, this is for your best as well. I withheld sight from the man born blind so that my glory could be revealed in him, and so that he and others could meet me as the God of sight and healing.[4] That man got to encounter me in a way most people never do. He met the God who knew him personally, cared deeply, had a purpose for his life from birth, and touched and healed him. I had his best in mind, along with the best for my Kingdom and others who would hear of his story and come to know me through it.

I also withheld my healing from Lazarus and allowed him to die in order that he and the world might come to know me as the resurrection and the life. It was for everyone's best interest, including his own, that I allowed him to die first so that all might see a fuller extent of my power and glory as I raised him from the dead. When I arrived late to Bethany, my lateness was an

---

[3] James 1:2-3
[4] John 9:3

act of love. I may have been late for a healing, but I was right on time for a resurrection. He experienced an encounter with me and my life-giving Spirit in a more intimate and real way than you can possibly imagine. I had his best in mind. I had the best for Mary and Martha, his grieving sisters, in mind. I had the best for the world in mind. I had the best for my Kingdom in mind.[5]

The story of Job is another great example of a time when I withheld my protection and blessings for a season for the sake of my name in the earth. But even with Job my withholding was ultimately for his good, as he encountered me in a way he never had before. (And then later he received a double portion, abundantly more than all he could ask or imagine!)[6] My purposes are always higher than yours. They are always filled with more goodness, wisdom, and love than you can see. Trust my heart! No good thing will I withhold from you."

* Breathing Exercises:

1. *Think about the areas of your life where you feel like God is withholding something good. Can you see that this withholding might be for your wholeness or for the sake of His Kingdom right now? If you're not sure, ask the Lord. Ask Him to give you insight into the situation from His perspective. And then* **listen**. *Write down anything He shares with you. Maybe He will give you a different reason not mentioned in this reading. That's great! These are not the only reasons God withholds from us—there are an infinite number of good and loving reasons that He withholds in different situations.*

---

[5] John 11:1-44
[6] Job 42:12-16

2. *Once He shares some of His reasons with you, take time to choose to believe His words and embrace His ways with trust and surrender. Allow your heart to rest in His goodness for the rest of the week. When you find yourself getting anxious and frustrated over the things you don't have, meditate on the goodness of God's heart towards you and remind yourself of the words He spoke to you. Believe His words and rest in the goodness of your Father who will never withhold any **good thing** from you, and is working on your behalf.*

The Best

*"I am the Lord your God, who teaches you what is **best for you**, who directs you in the way you should go. If only you had paid attention to my commands, your peace would have been like a river, your righteousness like the waves of the sea."*
Isaiah 48:17b-18

"Beloved, my heart wants what's best for you, and I am committed to your best. I desire the absolute best for you—not just mediocre, not just good—I want the best! I want what's best for **you**; not just what's best for me, my name, and my Kingdom. I do care about those things, but I simultaneously care deeply about what's best for you. Please don't let others convince you otherwise. I have your best interests in mind when I speak to you, ask things of you, lead you, and ordain all the days written for you. I am continually looking out for your best interests and I will never give you anything less than my best for you: that which is most life-giving, soul-fulfilling, and satisfying. My best will help you to become all that I created you to be, enter the deepest level of intimacy possible with me, and bring the most joy, depth, peace, character, and contentment into your heart and soul. Ultimately, Beloved, what's best for you is going to be what brings you closest to me. Because I AM what's best for you. The abundant life, fullness of joy, overflowing peace, and transforming love found in my presence are what's best for you.

Now, this doesn't mean that you will always experience my best for you. For though I yearn for your best, there is an adversary out to steal my best from you. He schemes day and night, looking for ways to deceive you and lead you astray from my best. He did it to Adam and Eve, he does it to you, and he does it to others in the world. Beloved, it breaks my heart to watch this happen. I hate watching my children stray from my commands and my best for them, causing deep pain for themselves and for others. Know that this pain was never my intention; it's simply a by-product of the free will I give you and the war between good and evil that you fight in each day, whether you realize it or not. But Beloved, even when you or others stray from my best, if you let me, I promise to take those mistakes and turn them into good—into a new best!

I am an expert at taking my children's mistakes and creating a new best out of the mess they've made. Take David for example—my best was never for him to commit adultery with Bathsheba, for her husband Uriah to be killed, or for thousands of Israelites to die as a consequence. David sinned and many lives were lost and damaged in the process. But he repented and I took his mistake and still used it for good for him and the world. For through his relationship with Bathsheba, I brought a son that continued the lineage that led to the birth of Christ![1] I brought the Savior of the world through a relationship that had strayed from my best. I redeemed it and created a new "best" out of the mess.

Beloved, I want the best for you in every area of your life. I want the husband who will be best for you; I want to bring him in the timing that will be best for you; I want you in the ministry that will be best for you; I want you in the living situation that will best for you; I want you in the country that will be best for you. In every situation, I want what is best for your soul and heart

---

[1] 2 Samuel 11-12

and I will direct you in the way you should go to experience it, but it's up to you to trust me and follow where I lead.

Pay attention to what I'm asking of you right now. Listen to what I'm saying, be sensitive to where I'm leading you, and open your heart to my teaching and commands for you. Trust me, you don't want to miss my best for you. My commands are the stepping stones that will lead you into my best, so pay special attention to them. Don't be like the Israelites who ignored my commands and set out to find the "best" on their own. They thought they knew better than I did. They didn't trust that my heart had their best in mind and that if they would choose to follow, I would lead them into the best.[2] If only they had paid attention to my commands, if only they had trusted my heart and my ways, their peace would have been like a river.[3]

That promise of peace still stands for my people today. If you will only trust my heart and follow my instructions, indescribable peace will flow throughout your entire being. There is a life-giving river of peace for you to tap into if you will listen to, believe, and obey my words. When you don't trust that I will provide the best for you, life becomes an endless, tiring struggle trying to arrange your own best in all areas of life. You don't have to carry that burden, my child. I promise to lead you into the best; you simply get to enjoy the adventure and mystery of it all as you receive my instructions and follow them step by step."

* Breathing Exercises:

---

[2] The story of the Israelites' journey with God and their struggle to trust Him as He leads them into the Promised Land and establishes them there can be read in Exodus-2 Samuel. A few great examples are in Exodus 16-17, Numbers 11, 13, 20, and 1 Samuel 8.
[3] Isaiah 48:18

1. *Is there an area of your life in which you don't believe that God has your best in mind? Is there a situation from the past that makes it difficult to believe that He cares about your best? Talk to Him about these situations. Ask Him to show you the subtle lies that the enemy is feeding you. Rebuke the lies and claim the truth of Isaiah 48:17-18.*

2. *What instruction is God giving you that you are reluctant to follow right now? His commands and guidance are **always** for your best. If you don't know what guidance He's giving you, ask Him! Make a commitment today to obey what He's asking of you. As you obey, you will step into His best for you and experience a life-giving river of peace.*

I Am For You!

*"If God is **for us**, who can be against us?" Romans 8:31b*

*"Since ancient times no one has heard, no ear has perceived, no eye has seen any God besides you, who **acts on behalf** of those who wait for Him." Isaiah 64:4*

*"The Lord be exalted, who **delights in the well-being of his servant**." Psalm 35:27b*

*"And we know that in all things God works for the **good** of those who love him, who have been called according to his purpose." Romans 8:28*

"Beloved, I delight in your well-being. I really do! I delight to see your heart, soul, mind, and body thrive. I want everything about you to be well and whole. I don't delight in your pain, loss, emptiness, lack, or suffering. You need to know this and rest in this truth. I am 100% committed to working **all** things together for your good and well-being. And Beloved, all things means **all things**! I will never stop working for your good in any circumstance of your life. I will never quit on you, give up on you, nor remove my hand that forever works on your behalf. No matter what others may do to you, what pain this broken world inflicts on you, or what mistakes you make, I will never stop working for your good in each and every situation.

I am a redeemer (an avenger; deliverer; one who purchases back all that's been lost) and am committed to redeeming every negative and painful situation in your life. I am a God who loves to bring beauty from ashes and life from death. I am the Great Restorer and Redeemer—the One who is seeking your good in and through every situation. Come and know me for the Redeemer I truly am.

Beloved, I want you to know that *I am for you!* It's true—I am 100% *for* you. I am for your well-being; I am for your future; I am for your marriage; I am for your character development; I am for your joy; I am for your peace; I am for you in the endeavors I have asked you to undertake for me. I am for your best in every aspect of your life.

So guess what that means? If I am for you, then you don't have to worry about being for yourself. Isn't that good news? I, the God of the universe, the One no power can stand up to—am for you. The Great I AM is for you, so who in the world can prevail against you? No one. It's impossible. Your destiny is secure. Your future is secure. My plans for you are secure. So relax and smile.

You don't have to be for yourself. You don't have to worry about looking out for your own best interests and arranging your circumstances. I've got you, Child. I'm fighting for you and I'm working for your good and well-being. I truly am a God who works on your behalf. In fact, I love working on your behalf; it's one of my greatest delights! So guess what you get to focus on? You get to live for me. You get to wake up and be *for me* each day. You are free to live for me and my Kingdom. Come enter this freedom from all worry and self-consumption; the freedom of knowing that I am working on your behalf and am committed to doing you good with all my heart and soul; the glorious freedom of living as one of my children!"

* Breathing Exercises:

1. *Where in your life do you need God to come in as the Great Redeemer (*an avenger; deliverer; one who purchases back all that's been lost)*? Where do you need Him to bring incredible good from a painful situation? What situation do you long to see Him work together for your good? Share this desire with Him. Ask Him to redeem it! Release it to Him and **believe** that He will act on your behalf in this situation. Trust Him to bring incredible good! Rejoice today in the mind-blowing goodness He is going to bring. Praise Him for all the good you know is coming from this situation. Stand on the promise in Romans 8:28 and sing throughout the day for the miracles He is sure to do.*

2. *Where in your life do you struggle to trust that God is for you? Hint: think of the areas of your life in which you tend to take things into your own control and feel that you must be "for yourself." Ask Him to help you surrender these areas to Him and trust that He is **for you** and will work on your behalf. Surrender control to Him and decide to live your day **for Him** since He has already promised that He is for you. Step into the glorious freedom of simply living each moment and day for Him, trusting that He will care for you.*

"It boggles the mind to try to imagine what it must mean if the God who made the planets and stars and galaxies and molecules and protons and neutrons and electrons **rejoices to do you good** with *all* his heart and with *all* his soul. If God is God *for you*, then *all* his omnipotence and *all* his omniscience are engaged *all* the time **to do good for you** in **all** the circumstances of your life."

—John Piper[1]

[1] John Piper, "God's Covenant with Abraham," sermon preached at Bethlehem Baptist Church, 4 December 1983.

FULFILLED DESIRES

I take pleasure in giving you the desires of your heart.

The Desires of Your Heart

*"Delight yourself in the Lord and **he will give you the desires of your heart**." Psalm 37:4*

*"You have granted him **the desire of his heart** and have not withheld the **request of his lips**." Psalm 21:2*

"My child, I want you to know that I take so much pleasure in giving you the desires of your heart. I really do! I placed those deep desires in you and I delight in fulfilling them. I didn't give them to you with the intention that they would remain unfulfilled forever. I put them there to drive you to your knees in prayer, to teach you to approach my throne with confidence, to ask me for them, to seek my heart, to draw you to me, and to bless and satisfy you by fulfilling them.

I am a God who loves to grant the request of your lips![1] I love the days that you approach my throne with confidence and vulnerably share the desires of your heart with me. I already know your desires, but I love hearing *you* share them with me. I love experiencing that type of intimate conversation with you. I love it when you trust me enough to share your deepest desires with me and believe in faith that I will grant them.

Your desires aren't evil, my child. You don't need to cover them up or suppress them, especially from me. Please don't ever think that you need to hide your desires from me. I gave many of

---

[1] Psalm 21:2

them to you and I want to dialogue with you about them and fulfill them for you. Let me help you understand something: desires come from two different sources—your sinful nature and my Spirit.

*"Those who live according to the sinful nature have their minds set on what **that nature desires**; but those who live in accordance with the Spirit have their minds set on what **the Spirit desires**. The mind of the sinful man is death, but the mind controlled by the Spirit is life and peace . . . You, however, are not controlled by the sinful nature but by the Spirit, if the Spirit of God lives in you."* **Romans 8:5-6,9a**

Beloved, the sinful nature is filled with desires that lead to lust, greed, selfishness, murder, idolatry, envy, sexual immorality, and a whole lot of other destructive and evil acts. These are *not* the desires I long to fulfill in you and I will in no way intervene to grant them. However, when you surrendered your life to me and invited my Spirit to fill you and take over, I began to awaken desires in you that are in line with my Kingdom, my heart, and my will for you. You are a new creation filled with my Spirit and when you seek my heart, and allow me to reign in you and control your mind, you can trust that the desires you experience are from me. Some desires come straight from my throne room! And if you're unsure, just ask me, "Lord is this desire from you?" I'm always happy to answer you.

I didn't create the feeling of hunger (physical, emotional, or spiritual) so that people would feel hungry all their lives. You feel physical hunger because I created your body to need food. The hunger is an indication that your body is lacking something for which it was created. The hunger is made to be satisfied and to bring you joy and contentment in that satisfaction. The feeling of hunger makes the joy of eating all the sweeter. The same goes for the hungers of your soul: your hunger for intimacy, belonging, purpose, meaning, and love. These hungers indicate that your soul is lacking something for which it was created, and I love coming in to fulfill these hungers and thirsts. Beloved, I AM the Bread of Life that satisfies your deepest hunger.[2] I AM the Living Water that takes away thirst altogether.[3] The desires of your heart aren't some cruel joke from me. I placed them in you that I might fill them. I am your life-giving source and the great I AM! Come to me, delight in me, and let me fill them."

* Breathing Exercises:

1. *Take some time to identify and write down the current desires of your heart. As you look at your list, ask the Lord to show you which desires stem from your sinful nature and which ones are from Him. If you are walking closely with the Lord, chances are that most of your desires are from Him. If you're not sure about one of them, think about what God's Word says about that desire. Is there any scripture that speaks against this type of desire? Is there any scripture that indicates this type of desire is from God? If you still aren't sure, ask the Lord to show you His perspective on that desire throughout the coming week (and then be ready for His answer that may come through the words of a friend, a book, the Bible, or a still quiet voice in your heart).*

2. *Why do you think God placed these desires in your heart? Do you think He did it as a cruel joke? Will you trust His declaration that He placed them there to draw you to Himself and to fulfill them? Spend some time seeking Him and asking Him for the desires of your heart. Ask for eyes to see how **He** wants to fulfill them.*

---

[2] John 6:35
[3] John 4:13

Ask for patience to trust in and wait on His timing. Ask Him to speak into these areas. Then listen. Write down anything you sense He is saying. Then trust Him. Trust His timing, His ways, His wisdom, and His love.

Delighting in Him

*"**Delight yourself in the Lord** and he will give you the desires of your heart." Psalm 37:4*

"My child, I *love* to give you the desires of your heart. This is true for the more general desires I've placed in your heart—things like love, intimacy, and purpose—but it's also true for the personal and specific desires that I've given you. I care about your desires for a husband, children, and to walk free from the fear of man. Let me speak into the husband area right now. Kierra, I do want to give you the desire of your heart for a husband. I do. I am so excited for him to find you and to bring you to each other. I am so excited for you to participate in this incredible union I have planned. But your job isn't to find him. Your job is to delight in me. Can you do that? Can you just delight in me right now and trust me to give you this desire?"

Yes, Lord, I will delight in you in every way I know how. Will you teach me the practice of delighting? That's one in which I'm not very trained. I'm quite skilled at worrying, analyzing, controlling, working, and serving. I'm definitely not an expert or specialist in delighting, but I want to be—I really do! I want to become a specialist in the art of delighting and treasuring. I want to sign up for the class, "Delighting in the Lord 101"! But I don't want it to stop at a basic course; I want to go deep. I want to continue to get my doctorate in this. Will you teach me, Lord? I'm ready to learn!

"Beloved, I'd be delighted to—I'm so glad you asked. This is one of my favorite courses to teach my children, and I wish more of them would recognize the importance of it. I'm hesitant to give you specific instructions because true delight never comes through the law, but I *will* share some practices and concepts to help you on your journey.

The first thing, Beloved, is that you need to slow down. It is very hard to delight in something or someone when you are on high speed all day. Savoring and enjoying something requires that you take the time to fully experience the gift of it. Beloved, I know this is counter-cultural, but I need you to slow down your pace. The way you eat your food is a great example. I desire for you to taste and savor your food, but most of the time you're in such a hurry that you don't even taste your meals. You either scarf them down so fast that you don't have time to take in the delightful flavor, or you try to multi-task while you eat and are too caught up in your other activity to notice the food. I know this may seem like an insignificant example to you, but it is a very accurate depiction of the rest of your life. Did you know that I specifically created saliva to begin the digestion process? It's true! You were created to savor the taste of food in your mouth for much longer than a second or two—this savoring time is key for healthy digestion! In the same way, savoring the moments and gifts in your day is key for spiritual health.

The second habit that's crucial to the art of delighting in me is that of being present. Beloved, you will never learn to delight in me without first learning to be present to me. My child, you are so rarely present to me, my workings, and my gifts throughout the day. You're so focused on where you have to be in an hour that you miss the gift of where I have you right now. I am continually pouring out expressions of my undying love for you, but you are rarely present enough to enjoy or recognize them. When you learn to live present to me, you will find yourself automatically delighting in me throughout the day. There is so much about myself and my workings in your life that will ignite pure delight in you!

Beloved, my final instructions for you are simple: **enjoy** me and the day! Focus on enjoying all aspects and gifts in your day. Enjoy your drive to work, the warmth of the sun on your face, the refreshing glass of ice water on your table, and the goofy humor of the clerk at the grocery store. And as you do all this, enjoy me! Enjoy my creation in the flowers outside your window and the people you meet. Enjoy spending your day with me in everything we do together. Enjoy my companionship and who I am. If you want, pick a different aspect of my nature to intentionally enjoy each day. Be intentional about focusing on me throughout the day and enjoying my presence. You will find yourself delighting in me in no time!"

* Breathing Exercises:

The exercises today are simple. Just follow the Lord's three practices above to help you learn how to delight in Him!

1. *Slow down and savor the day. Slow your pace as you eat, drive, work, shop, and visit with others. Savor the smells, the taste, the person, the music, the activity, and the gift of each moment.*
2. *Seek to be present in each moment today. Don't live an hour from now; live in **this** moment.*
3. *Enjoy God this day! Pick one aspect of His nature to particularly enjoy today. Maybe it's His creativity or maybe it's His kindness or maybe His beauty, faithfulness, consistency, or generosity. Pick one aspect to enjoy today, and then pick a new one tomorrow, and so on for the rest of the week.*

The Proper Time

"The eyes of all look to you, and you give them their food **at the proper time**. *You open your hand and* **satisfy the desires of every living thing**. *The Lord is righteous in all his ways and loving toward all he has made. The Lord is near to all who call on him, to all who call on him in truth. He* **fulfills the desires of those who fear him**." *Psalm 145:15-19a*

"Beloved, I love giving you the desires of your heart, but timing is everything. There is both a proper time for your desires to be met, as well as an improper time. Please trust my timing. It's like the gift of sex. I've put a desire in men and women for sex—it is a desire that I created in them. But there is a proper and improper time for that desire to be fulfilled. Before marriage is an improper time. Only after marriage will the fulfillment of that desire be all that I created and intended it to be. Only in the safety, unity, and commitment of marriage will the fulfillment of that desire be truly complete. This is because there is something deeper to the desire than the physical longing. There is a spiritual and emotional component to the desire that will only truly be met in the safety and security of the marriage covenant.

So can you please trust my timing for the fulfillment of all the different desires in your heart right now? I know that they are strong and you want them met **now**, but if I were to fulfill them now they wouldn't be everything you're hoping for. They wouldn't fulfill you the way they will in my perfect timing. Beloved, I really do have your best interests at heart when I ask you to wait for the fulfillment of some of these desires.

I don't ask my engaged children to wait for sex because I'm cruel or unsympathetic. I ask them to wait because I love them too much to let them settle for less than my best. I created the perfect fulfillment for that desire, and I want to lead them into an experience of *that* and nothing less. This is true for every desire I have given you.

Will you look to me to fulfill your desires instead of trying to fulfill them yourself in your own timing? Call on me, Beloved, and bring your desires to me. I am near to all who call on me and I fulfill the desires of those who fear me (who are caught up in awe and reverence of me).[1] Don't spend your days fearing that your desires will remain unfulfilled. Fear will never get you anywhere. You can worry and fret and take things into your own hands, but it will accomplish nothing other than producing some tension headaches and gray hairs. Look to me! Magnify me! Call on me! Delight in me! Trust me! Focus on these activities and I will give you the desires of your heart. My gifts won't always look like what you are expecting, but if you will stay open to my ways and wisdom, you will experience the fulfillment of your desires even in unexpected ways. Trust me, Beloved; I am faithful to all my promises and loving toward all that I have made."[2]

* Breathing Exercises:

1. *Do you spend more time worrying and thinking about your desires or bringing them before the Lord? Which do you magnify more: your situations or the Lord? Reflect on these questions and confess your worry and idolatry to God. Ask for forgiveness and ask Him to help you take every thought captive and make it obedient to*

---

[1]   Psalm 145:15-19
[2]   Psalm 145:13

Him. Bring your desires before Him again and commit to praying about them instead of worrying or trying to fulfill them yourself throughout the week. Call on Him, center your attention on Him, seek His heart, and trust His perfect timing.

2. *Is there a deep desire in your heart that seems long in coming? Does God seem to be late on this one? Bring your hurt and confusion to Him. He can take it and longs for you to share your heart with Him. Share your disappointment and be honest with Him. Ask Him to show you what He's up to in this situation, because He is **always** up to something and that something is **always** for your good. Ask to see things from His perspective. What does He want to develop in you? Would the fulfillment of this desire be incomplete if He brought it now? Listen to His words and write them down. Memorize Psalm 145:15-16. Write it on a card and carry it around with you throughout the week. Choose to believe it! On the back of the card, write John 7:6 and let it also encourage you throughout your days.*

FULLY GENEROUS

I love lavishing my generosity on you.

My Generous Heart

*"He who did not spare His own Son, but gave him up for us all—how will he not also, along with him, **graciously give us all things?**" Romans 8:32*

*"And do not set your heart on what you will eat or drink; do not worry about it. For the pagan world runs after all such things, and your Father knows that you need them. But seek His kingdom, and these things will be given to you as well. Do not be afraid, little flock, for your Father has been **pleased to give you the Kingdom**." Luke 12:29-32*

*"And my God will meet **all your needs** according to his glorious riches in Christ Jesus." Philippians 4:19*

"Beloved, my heart towards you is so generous! I love blessing you with all the riches of my Kingdom and giving you far more than you can possibly receive or take in. I love to pour out blessing after blessing and measure after measure of my love, gifts, and presence to you. I gave my life for you; there's nothing else I would hold back. I find so much delight in giving. One of my greatest joys is loving you and giving to you. You can't stop me from giving—it's just in my nature; it's who I am.

So often you come to me with a lot of guilt in asking for requests. Deep down you think that I don't like hearing requests or giving out gifts. But when you come to know my generous nature, you will know that I absolutely *love* giving gifts! I like to give over and above what you would ever ask or dream for.

I don't just settle for the minimum; I want to give you the best. That is my joy. My heart overflows with passionate love for you and in that overflow, my generosity pours out. I can't stop it; my generosity is a gushing river.

Don't you see it in my death? There's nothing I wouldn't give for you. *Nothing.* I would go to any length to give you what you need and to pour out my generous love on you. There is no limit to how far I would go nor how much I would give. No limit my child, no limit.

I am the most generous being you will ever meet. The generosity that you see in others is but a drop in the ocean of my generosity; it doesn't even begin to compare. You can think of the most generous person you know, then multiply the depth of their generosity by a million and that still doesn't compare to *my* generosity. And Beloved, my generosity is pure. **I simply love to give.** I don't give to receive anything back from you. I don't give to manipulate my people or gain from them in any way. I simply give for the joy of giving. I give because the overwhelming love in my heart won't allow me to do otherwise. My love for you compels me. I *must* give. I can't dam up my generosity; the depth of my love for you is an open and continuous gateway that will never shut. It doesn't matter what you do, my love for you will never end and my generous nature will never change. This is simply who I am. I am a lover and giver—generous by nature and never changing. Come and know me for the generous giver that I am."

* Breathing Exercises:

1. *When you think of God, do you think of a generous, joyful giver? If not, how do you picture Him? Why do you think that is? Take some time to meditate on Romans 8:32:*

"He who did not spare His own Son, but gave him up for us all—how will he not also, along with him, graciously give us all things?" Romans 8:32

*Read it slowly a couple of times. Then take some time to picture Jesus' death. Marvel at His generosity as He gives His life for you. Though it was horrific and painful, He gladly gave it for you. For the joy set before Him (the relationship He would get with **you**), He endured the cross.[1] Now take some time to picture the Father during the crucifixion. See the pain in His eyes as He generously gives His Son for you. See the depth of His love and generosity towards you. See Him for the loving giver that He is. Now go back and re-read Romans 8:32 a few more times. Let the truth of this verse sink into your heart.*

2. *Enjoy your generous King today! Notice His generosity around you. Ask Him to help you get to know Him as the giver that He is. Then as He pours out His generosity onto you, seek to be a vessel that generously pours it out onto others. Freely receive from Him and then freely give to others. May they experience the generosity of God through you. Introduce them to your generous King!*

---

[1] Hebrews 12:2b

Enjoying My Good Gifts

*"Ask and it will be given to you; seek and you will find; knock and the door will be opened to you. For everyone who asks receives; he who seeks finds; and to him who knocks, the door will be opened. Which of you, if his son asks for bread, will give him a stone? Or if he asks for a fish, will give him a snake? If you, then, though you are evil, know how to give good gifts to your children, **how much more will your Father in heaven give good gifts to those who ask him!**" Matthew 7:7-11*

"Beloved, I am a gift giver. This is who I am. I *love* giving good gifts to my children; I absolutely love it! It brings me pure delight and is one of my favorite things to do. And I'm really good at it—I know how to give the best gifts imaginable! Because I know you better than you know yourself, I know your desires better than you do, and I know what you need at a far deeper level than you ever will. I know the exact gift that you need at each moment, and I love showing up and giving it. I love watching you receive it, enjoy it, and find deep satisfaction from it. I love watching your mouth and heart smile with delight. I love bringing joy to you; I love surprising you; I love being generous towards you; I love overflowing your cup; and I love blessing you more than you will ever know.

I wish you would love being blessed by me more. I would love for you to enjoy my gifts as much as I enjoy giving them to you. I often get so excited to give you one of my perfect gifts, but you are too busy to notice it, you feel guilty for enjoying it, or you don't seem to really care. That's a bummer to me. I put so much love and thought into the gifts I give you. I put my heart into them and I'm giving you a piece of my heart when I give them to you, so for you to disregard them nonchalantly is for you to treat me and my heart towards you nonchalantly. It's a form of rejection to me and my overflowing love for you. I give my gifts to make you smile and to bring joy and delight to your heart. So smile, my girl. Receive my love gifts and smile! It's okay to allow my gifts to bring you joy. I want them to. It doesn't mean you're neglecting me or looking for joy in other places. By enjoying my gifts, you are enjoying me and my incredible heart towards you.

Beloved, enjoying me doesn't have to mean alone time with me on your knees in your bedroom. I want you to enjoy me and my gifts in everything you do throughout the day. Enjoying me can be going for a walk and enjoying the sunshine on your face and the wildflowers I planted. It can be enjoying a good cup of tea with a friend and treasuring the friendship I've given you. For you, it can be dancing. I made you to dance and I love watching you dance. And you know what? I love watching you dance even when you're not thinking about me. I don't expect you to be thinking about me every second of the day, so please stop feeling guilty and quit trying so hard. The pressure you put on yourself is stealing the joy of the moment and the gift in front of you. It still brings me glory and delight to watch you enjoy a gift even if you're not 100% conscious of me at that moment in time.

A dad finds joy in watching his daughter excitedly ride her new bike, even if she isn't constantly thanking him every second— trying to remember the bike was a gift from him and she should be grateful for it. If she stopped every minute to thank her dad again, he would say, "Honey, just go play and enjoy your bike. You don't have to keep thanking me. You are welcome for the gift and now I want you to go enjoy it."

Beloved, this is true for every gift I give you throughout your days. I just want you to enjoy them. Yes, thank me for them and let the fact that they are a gift from my heart draw you into a deeper experience of my love. But you don't have to be so serious about that. You don't have to worry each day if you're thanking me enough or remembering me enough. Yes, I love to hear thanksgiving regularly roll off your tongue, but you live under so much pressure to thank me that you often miss enjoying the gift. I'm telling you right now, "You are welcome." Now have fun and enjoy my gifts. More than anything, I want to watch you have fun with them. Have fun with the friends I give you, your co-workers, your husband, and your family. Yes, seek me together, draw closer to me with each other, minister together, and sharpen one another, but in all of this, ***have fun***!

I am a fun God! I don't know where you got it in your head that I'm so serious. I'm definitely not as serious as you. I love laughter. I love fun surprises. I love enjoying my creation. I love having fun and playing with my children. I love celebrating! I actually ordained yearly feasts of celebration for my people Israel, as well as whole years for celebration.[1] I'm inviting you to celebrate. Come join the celebration of life! Let your child-like heart come out and have some fun with me and with the amazing gifts I'm giving to you. Did you forget rule #1 in swing dancing? Have fun![2] I want to have fun with you. I want you

---

[1] Exodus 23:14, Leviticus 25:10-12

[2] God teaches me much about life with Him through swing dancing. I want to learn to follow His lead throughout the day and dance with Him in the same way I learn to follow the lead of my partner. At my first dance lesson, we learned the top two rules for swing dancing. Rule #1: Have Fun! Rule #2: Stay on the beat. Both have proven to be quite powerful for me as I learn to dance with God throughout my days, enjoying Him and the dance and learning to stay on *His* beat.

to have fun with others. Have fun today, Beautiful! Have fun driving to work. Have fun in the office getting to involve others in my exciting mission. Have fun with your co-workers. Have fun in massage class. That's your job today. Have fun and enjoy my gifts!"

** Breathing Exercise:*

1. *Have **fun** today! That's it. Break out of your seriousness and go have some fun with the Lord and the people He's put in your life. Whatever is on your plate for the day, determine to have fun doing it and invite others to have fun as well. Here are just a few ideas:*

   - *Play fun music (on your drive, as you're cleaning, etc. Music can make any task more fun)*
   - *Dance to the music in your car. Don't worry about what other people think*
   - *Make your work a game and promise yourself a fun reward when you finish a certain amount of it*
   - *Take a five minute break to twirl on the grass or do cartwheels*
   - *Invite your co-workers to take a 5-minute goofy break: have a wheelbarrow race, watch a funny clip on YouTube, tell your most embarrassing moment stories.*
   - *Play a game with your friends or family when you get home from work*
   - *Go on some swings*
   - *Lie in the grass and enjoy the sun*
   - *Take fun pictures with your camera*

The Gift of My Spirit

*"If you then, though you are evil, know how to give good gifts to your children, how much more will your Father in heaven **give the Holy Spirit** to those who ask him!" Luke 11:13*

*"For God **gives** the Spirit **without limit**." John 3:34b*

"Beloved, as much as I love giving you a wide variety of gifts, my all-time favorite gift to bestow is the Holy Spirit. This gift tops them all and my heart gets so excited to pour it out on those who desire it and ask me for it. More than anything, this is what you need and what will bring true fulfillment to your heart. This is the greatest gift I can give you. When I give you my Spirit, I give you my very being and everything that fills my essence. When I give you my Spirit, I give you the fullness of my love, joy, peace, comfort, wisdom, power, and strength. And Beloved, I give my Spirit without limit! There is **no limit** to how much of my Spirit you can receive, so don't ever settle with the amount you have. Keep asking for more, keep making room for more, keep hungering for more, and I will continue to give and give until you are soaked to levels you never dreamed possible. *"Ask and you will receive, and your joy will be complete!"*[1]

You have no idea how incredible this gift is. It's a winning lotto ticket placed in your hands that you still haven't cashed in. There is an unlimited supply of everything your heart truly longs for, right at your fingertips. To cash in, you just need to ask. That's

---

[1] John 16:24b

it. Ask for *more*. Then ask for more again. Then more. And more. This is one gift for which you can always be greedy. I will never tire of hearing you ask for more of my Spirit. **Never.** Your cries for more are music to my heart; a fragrant aroma in my throne room. I love filling you with my Spirit. I want you to walk around intoxicated with it. I want you to be totally undone by it. I want you to be saturated and overflowing with it! *"Do not get drunk on wine, which leads to debauchery. **Instead,** be filled with the Spirit."*[2] Get drunk on me! It's way better than any intoxication from alcohol. I will fill you with uncontainable joy and peace far beyond what you can imagine.

Oh Beloved, this gift is so good, it's actually better than my physical presence. You have a gift far greater than the disciples ever had while I walked with them on this earth. That's why it was good for them that I went to my Father. Until I left them, I couldn't send the Counselor (my Spirit) to live in them.[3] It was far greater for them to live with the Counselor *in them,* than to simply walk next to me. I left the earth so that I could give you this great gift—my very Presence living in you every second of every day. My Spirit now lives in you to comfort you, guide you, speak through you, work miracles through you, breathe life through you, and fill you with unexplainable peace, joy, and love.

Beloved, there is no end to how much I want my Spirit to increase in you. Understand the truth of the prophesy in Isaiah 9:6: *"And he will be called Wonderful Counselor, Mighty God, Everlasting Father, Prince of Peace. Of the **increase** of his government and peace there will be no end."* Beloved, this is true in the world and in your life. There is no end to how much I want my reign and peace to increase in your life. Each day

---

[2] Ephesians 5:18
[3] John 16:6

there is more! Get excited, Beloved. I am a God of immeasurably more and a never-ending increase. So ask, seek, receive, enjoy, and share!"

* **Breathing Exercises:**

1. *Set aside 30 minutes to ask for and receive more of God's Spirit. Find a place where you can be completely alone, uninterrupted, and undistracted. Make sure it's a place that you are free to pray, cry, sing, and communicate with God as loudly and freely as you desire.*

   Start by thanking him for the promises in Luke 11:13, and John 3:34 (at the beginning of this reading). Thank Him over and over again. Let incredible gratefulness rise up in your heart as you realize the power of these promises. Give thanks and tell God how incredible this gift is. Enter into a place of deep gratitude and thanksgiving. Try to spend at least 10 minutes just thanking Him.

   Then begin to ask. Ask for more of His Spirit. Share and ask from the bottom of your heart and keep asking. As you ask, allow yourself to receive anything that He begins pouring out into you. He sends His Spirit with many gifts and you will experience them in different forms. You may start weeping. You may be filled with a slow peace that you can't explain. You may start giggling (if this happens, let yourself laugh! Laugh out loud and receive the gift of joy that He is giving you). You may start praying in another language that is foreign to you. You may feel tingling throughout your body. You may feel heat. You may see a vision. You may hear words in your spirit. Or you may not "feel" anything. All of these are okay. Give yourself the freedom to fully experience what God is giving you. **Receive** *the Spirit that He is* *pouring into you. And if you don't "feel" anything out of the ordinary, don't worry! He doesn't always come with tangible displays. But you can trust that He delights to hear your request and He **will** come to you and fill you. You may not notice until you are at work later in the day and respond differently to a difficult co-worker. You may notice an unusual peace and calm in situations that usually rile you up. Don't worry about how God is filling you right now—just trust that He is!*

2. *Begin to pray Isaiah 9:6 over every area of your life. "Of the increase of his government and peace there will be no end." Pray for an increase of His government and peace in your relationships, your finances, your work, your marriage, your ministry, your home, etc . . .*

    Commit to making this request for more of His Spirit an ongoing, consistent part of your days and weeks! Never stop asking for more—the amount He wants to give you is limitless!

A FULL CUP

I love to overflow your cup.

An Overflowing Cup

*"You prepare a table before me in the presence of my enemies.
You anoint my head with oil; **my cup overflows**."*
Psalm 23:5

*"For in Christ all the fullness of the Deity lives in bodily form,
and you have been given **fullness** in Christ, who is the head
over every power and authority." Colossians 2:9-10*

*"And God placed all things under his feet and appointed him
to be head over everything for the church, which is his body,
the fullness of Him who **fills everything in every way**."*
Ephesians 1:22-23

"Oh Beloved, I am neither a glass half-empty **nor** a glass half-full God. In me, your glass is always filled to the brim and overflowing. I am a God of fullness. I created you for fullness, and fullness is what I offer you each day of your life. Whatever you need, I have in overflowing abundance and I want to offer this abundance to you. I am an overflowing fountain and if you come to stand under me, I will always overflow your cup until you too become an overflowing fountain for others.

My love, you will never be able to fill your own cup to overflowing. I am the only one who can bring this type of fullness to you. Many people are walking around with half-empty glasses because they don't trust me to fill them and are trying to fill their cup themselves. But they're filling it with all the wrong things—things that won't actually *fill* their cup.

Let's pretend you have an empty cup in front of you and you proceed to "fill" it with five stones. At first glance, the rocks may look impressive and the cup may look full, but is it? In reality, it is nowhere near full. There is still a lot of empty space between the rocks. This is what happens in life when you try to "fill" your cup with things besides me. It may look impressive at first, but you and I both know there is still a great deal of emptiness in your life. *My* fullness, the water of life that I give, is the only thing that can truly fill every nook and cranny of your cup until it begins to overflow! And oh, how it will then refresh and spill over to those around you.

Marriage isn't going to fill your cup, my child. Living in another country isn't going to fill your cup. Those are rocks that may take up space, but won't actually *fill* your cup. There will still be empty spaces and you're going to be disappointed and frustrated. Let all the richness of my presence fill your cup so that you can thrive and overflow *now*. Then when you add the rocks of marriage or overseas ministry, those rocks will be placed into a cup already overflowing with the water of life, and will simply make that cup overflow more.

Beloved, you can overflow at any stage of life because I am enough to fill you beyond capacity no matter what other "rocks" are filling your cup. If it's just you and me, and I am the only one filling your cup with the pure, heavenly water of life, you will be a gorgeous, life-giving fountain that displays my glory and runs over to bless those around you. And later in life, when your cup is filled with my intoxicating presence plus a husband and family and ministry to the nations, I will continue to fill you to overflowing as a display of my nature and glory to those around you. Can you see how your cup can overflow in any and every situation? This was the secret Paul was talking about when he said, "I have learned the secret of being content in any and every situation, whether well fed or hungry, whether living in plenty or in want. I can do everything through him who gives me strength."[1]

I want to overflow your cup in every season and situation in life. I want to overflow it in the presence of your enemies and in seasons of victory, in times of deep pain and times of inexpressible joy, in America and in Africa. Whatever the situation and whoever's presence you're in, I can and want to overflow your cup!"

Lord, I want to learn this secret! I want my testimony to be, "I have learned the secret to fullness in any and every situation, whether single or married, whether living in America or Africa, whether waking up to a large or small to-do list; the Lord is my portion and He overflows my cup!"

*Will you teach me? I guess when Paul says that he **learned** this secret, it means that this is going to be a process. I'm not going to get it overnight. That's okay—I'll be patient. I'm willing and excited to embark on the journey of learning this secret so that this can truly be my heartfelt testimony and actual experience.*

"Yes, Beloved, I will teach you and lead you into the experience of this truth as you continue to sit at my feet, listen to my words, and allow me to fill you with myself. I will be your portion, and your cup *will* overflow!"

* Breathing Exercise:

1. *Go outside and collect five to ten small rocks. Write on them the things with which you have been trying to "fill your cup" and the things that you are hoping will "fill*

---

[1] Philippians 4:12b-13

*your cup" in the future. Get a glass and put your rocks in it. As you look at the empty spaces in the glass, talk to the Lord about the empty spaces in your life. Confess the areas of your life where you have looked to other things to fill you instead of God. Confess your idolatry. Now fill the glass with water. As you watch the water fill every nook and cranny, ask the Lord to fill your life with His life-giving water—His Spirit! Share with Him your desire for **Him** to be your portion in any and every situation, for **Him** to be the One who continually overflows your cup. Leave the glass in a place where it can remind you of this lesson for the rest of the week.*

Nothing Do I Lack

*"The Lord is my shepherd, **I shall not be in want**."*
Psalm 23:1

"Beloved, I want you to come into a deep understanding of the truth that I am your shepherd and with me as your shepherd, you *do not* lack. This can be your testimony in any season of life. This can be your actual experience and biggest reality no matter what else is going on. You live with such a poverty mindset each day, always thinking you're lacking something. Whether it's a husband, time during the day, direction for the next season, financial security, or something as small as a cute outfit for the night—you are continually focused on what you "don't have." But I will always supply everything that you need for each moment, be it companionship, wisdom, provision, a garment of praise to wear for the evening, or my peace. I will always provide daily bread for you. Your heart doesn't believe this truth yet, but it can and it must in order for you to enter the joy and abundance that I long to characterize your life."

Lord, I hear what you are saying, but I struggle to fully believe your words. I understand that the Bible says that with you as our shepherd, we won't lack, but the state of so many lives in this world seems to contradict that for me. I know that 30,000 people around the world are going to die from starvation today, and I believe that many of them are Christians. Nothing do they lack? Sorry Lord, but in my own human wisdom, that seems like a bunch of baloney. Obviously they lacked—their lack was so great that they died from it. I have a lot of trouble reconciling Psalm 23:1 with this reality. Please help me understand.

After praying this prayer, the Lord began to open my eyes to the difference between true lack and perceived lack. I still don't have all the answers, but a conversation last year with my Kenyan friend, Betty, brought a lot of insight into these truths for me.

As Betty and I walked down the dirt roads of her village one day, I seized the moment to ask her my favorite question. "Betty, what has God been teaching you lately?" With a radiant smile and sparkling eyes, she answered, "That He is truly my shepherd." She went on . . .

"I've been reading Psalm 23 for the past six months and I still can't contain the joy that fills me when I read it. Imagine, Kierra, the Lord is *my* shepherd! He's my personal shepherd and with Him as my shepherd I never lack. He knows just where to lead me, how to provide for me, and how to care for me—He knows every detail of my life. And for sure, my cup overflows! Every day I am drinking from the overflow of God's blessings that run down the side of my cup (she took my water bottle to demonstrate how she drinks from the side as the blessings keep overflowing). I don't know why He keeps blessing me like this—He's such a wonderful shepherd. You know, I think I might be His favorite."

My heart wondered at her words and the glow on her face because from an earthly perspective, none of these words make sense: HIV positive, a single mom, no real source of income, and living in a small mud hut with her aging, sick mother and her 3-year old niece (who she's taken in as her own daughter), Betty spends most days feeling sick and hungry as she faithfully provides testing, counseling, and encouragement to others infected with HIV. *Nothing does she lack? Her cup overflows? Overflows with what?* I decided to ask.

"Betty, I know that you don't have much food in your home and you often go hungry. I know that you don't have a husband with whom to walk this journey and to provide for your children. I know that you feel sick much of the time. So how can you say so joyfully that you lack nothing? What is your cup overflowing with?"

She smiled at me as if she knew a great secret that I should also know by now. "For sure, there are days when there is no food in the home but I don't worry. It's those days that I pray to my God and say, 'Lord, this is your time. This is your time to come through as my shepherd. It is for you to provide for me today.' And for sure, He always does. He **always** provides. Sometimes He provides food, but other times He just provides Himself and His love and joy and peace. My cup overflows every day with more love, joy, and peace than I can contain. It overflows with my God, my shepherd."

Wow. Betty's heartfelt words pierced my own heart that afternoon as they destroyed my previous understanding of "lack." Maybe she lacked health and food but her heart and soul lacked nothing that they needed to live in the fullness of God. She had Him and He was, and is, and forever will be, enough. He is a perfect shepherd, committed to meeting our heart and soul's every need. There are thousands of people in the U.S. who will never lack for any material possession they desire, but they don't know Betty's shepherd, and consequently, lack more than she ever will. They lack the radiance of her countenance, the deep contentment and trust in her eyes, the confident assurance she walks in each day, the deep, all-consuming peace in her heart, and her hope of heaven. They lack the joy that comes from Betty's assurance that she's one of God's favorites. It's true, Betty is one of His favorites and she lives in the light of His favor each day of her life. But it's true for each of us as well; I too am loved as His favorite and can live in the light of that favor if only I recognize it each day. You are His favorite as well, and He loves you and delights in you more than you can possibly imagine! May we, like Betty, recognize and drink from the overflow of our cups today, for truly He is our shepherd and in Him we lack nothing!

** Breathing Exercise:*

1. *Do you focus more on what you have or what you don't have? Do you believe that you are lacking certain things necessary for abundant, full life? Talk to the Lord about those things. Then ask Him to give you a revelation of how He **is** providing for you as your shepherd. Thank Him for these things and for His incredible provision. Determine for the rest of the week to focus your eyes on what the Lord **is** providing you, rather than what you feel you are lacking. For the Lord is your shepherd and there is nothing that you lack today for abundant, overflowing life! Tap into the gifts He is giving you!*

FULLY WHOLE

I am committed to your wholeness.

The Process

*"O house of Israel, can I not do with you as this potter does?"
declares the Lord. "Like **clay in the hand of the potter**, so
are you in my hand, O house of Israel." Jeremiah 18:6*

*"Consider it pure joy, my brothers, whenever you face trials
of many kinds, because you know that the testing of your
faith develops perseverance. Perseverance must finish its work
so that you may be **mature and complete, not lacking
anything**." James 1:2-4*

"My child, I knit you together in your mother's womb with incredible plans for you and dreams of the person you would develop into. I saw the completed picture then and I still see it now. I **love** who I've made you to be. You get so frustrated that you're not the person you want to be yet. But Beloved, it's okay. You're exactly who I created you to be today, and I am pleased with you today. This whole thing was meant to be a process. I still have so much planned for your development, wholeness, and beauty. And I am so excited about it! I see the final picture (a radiant, trusting child, mature and complete, not lacking in anything) and I'm committed to seeing you through to this end. I, who began a good work in you, will carry it on to completion.[1]

I am a joy-filled potter who finds such delight in shaping you into the vessel I created you to be. I love each step of the potting

---

[1] Philippians 1:6

113

process, especially as you submit to my caring touch and allow yourself to be pliable clay in my hands. You must trust that you are pleasing to me in every step of the journey. When the potter is half-way through the sculpting process, he is never frustrated at the clay for not being a shining pot yet. The clay is in the exact form it should be at that point of the process. So it is with you, Beloved. You are right where you should be at this point of the process. Don't be so hard on yourself. Join my delight in each step of the journey.

Trust my leading and shaping; my plans for you along this journey are extremely intentional. I know the woman I'm forming you into. Everything I place in your path and every situation I lead you through is working toward this purpose. I know your weaknesses and I know exactly how to strengthen them. Don't worry about the areas in which you still feel you're lacking. It's okay. I see them too and am committed to helping you grow in each of these areas. I have a brilliant plan for your life and my hands are expert potter's hands. Trust me, my child, I am a master creator. Maturity, completion, and wholeness don't happen overnight. They are developed on a journey that I created to last a lifetime. And, oh, what a beautiful journey it is!"

* Breathing Exercises:

1. *Which area of your personality or character are you most hard on yourself about? What does Satan most condemn and accuse you about?*

   Now on the flip side, can you see how God has been working on this area in your life? Can you see ways that you have grown in it? If you have accepted Christ as your

Savior, there is no condemnation for you now.[2] God is bringing you through a daily journey of sanctification as He continues to mold and shape you into the vessel He created you to be.

*Picture yourself as that jar on His potter's wheel that is still in process. Ask God for a picture of how **He** sees you and where you are in the journey. Rejoice at where you are in the process. Rejoice that you're exactly where you should be today. Rejoice that you are on His potter's wheel and that **He** who began a good work in you will carry it on to completion. Walk free today—free from guilt and self-condemnation. Live in freedom as a deeply loved vessel in progress.*

2. *Is there a relationship you are struggling with right now? Is there someone with whom you are bitter, angry, annoyed, or frustrated? They too are a work in progress, a vessel on their way toward wholeness and completion. The Lord is just as committed to their wholeness as He is to yours, and He finds deep joy and delight in the vessel He is shaping them into. Ask Him for the grace to accept where they are in their own process as He slowly molds and shapes them. Ask to see what He is lovingly doing in their character and life, and then rejoice. Rejoice in the loving Potter who is taking each of you on a journey toward wholeness and who is infinitely patient with both of you.*

---

[2] Romans 8:1

Your Destiny

*"For those God foreknew he also **predestined to be conformed to the likeness of his Son**." Romans 8:29a*

*"For he will be like a refiner's fire or a launder's soap. He will sit as a refiner or purifier of silver; he will **purify the Levites** and **refine them like gold and silver**." Malachi 3:2b-3*

*"I am the true vine, and my Father is the gardener. He cuts off every branch in me that bears no fruit, while every branch that does bear fruit **he prunes so that it will be even more fruitful**." John 15:1-2*

"Beloved, do you know what I destined you for? It's not a comfortable life, it's not what the world would call a "happy" life, and it's definitely not an easy life. No, Beloved, I predestined you to be conformed to the image of my Son. This is your destiny! My plans for your life and character development are purposed to lead you into your ultimate destiny of reflecting the likeness of Christ in this world. Of course, you'll reflect Christ in your own Kierra way. I don't want you to lose your Kierra-isms. I love those about you—those unique parts of your personality that only you have. But I created you to ultimately reflect the character and likeness of Christ through all your unique Kierra attributes.

You have a choice: you can either allow the situations in your life to help shape you into the likeness of Christ, or you can fight, complain, get frustrated, and try to take things into your own hands. Allowing yourself to be molded and shaped is never easy or comfortable. It's often painful to be pushed and prodded, especially when sensitive areas are dug into. But I have kind potter's hands, hands anointed for healing. As I shape and mold you, I will always do so with the utmost gentleness, wisdom, love, compassion, and care. There will be seasons when I bring you into the refiner's fire. It will be painful, my girl—painful for both of us. But it is this heat that will burn away the impurities in you, leaving nothing but pure and radiant gold!

There will also be times when I have to prune and cut off parts of you.[1] I must slowly work to chip off everything in you that does not reflect the image of Christ. As painful as that cutting process will be, it will result in complete joy and freedom, for the parts of you that must be pruned are only weighing you down and holding you back. They are bondage, and your deliverance from them will be *life* for you and this world. Their removal will allow you to walk freely in my fullness as the true vessel I created you to be. This fullness will allow the world to see a reflection of me that they desperately need; to see me for whom I truly am.

People go through all sorts of painful treatments in order to attain outer beauty: waxing, surgeries, tattoos, laser treatments, starving themselves—the list goes on and on. People will withstand just about any painful process to gain the image they want. Well, what about the treatments necessary to portray *my* image? Are you willing to withstand the discomfort and pain? I promise you, Beloved, if you say "Yes", the breathtaking inner beauty that I will develop in you will be far greater than anything you can imagine. You will shine with a supernatural, glorious, world-changing beauty—a beauty that will draw all men to me as you reflect me to the world. And the great thing

---

[1] John 15:2

about my beauty is that it only increases as you age and as you submit to more and more of my plans and molding. The treatments won't always be fun or pleasant, but they will bring more good, joy, peace, healing, and wholeness than you can possibly imagine—both for you and for the world!

I know it's hard right now. I know you hate the "waiting" treatments I'm taking you through. But without the waiting, you will never develop the beautiful quality of patience. Without the waiting, you will only amount to a shallow, spoiled girl with no depth or character. I know it's hard to trust—that you want to *see* instead of hear the words "trust me". But it's in these seasons of learning to trust without seeing that I am able to develop the beautiful virtue of faith in you. It is in seasons requiring extreme trust that you get to know me for the God that I truly am, and I get to reveal myself to you in deeper ways than you could ever dream. These seasons are necessary for you to know me intimately and deeply and to help the world get to know me intimately and deeply. Beloved, submit to my workings in you, and not only will you be blessed, but through you all nations of the world will be blessed.[2] Submit to my workings and enter your destiny!"

* Breathing Exercises:

1. *Quiet your heart and mind and prepare to do some honest soul-searching. Ask God to reveal the true desires of your heart to you. Don't gloss over these questions. Think deeply about them, for they are of utmost importance.*

   - *Do you want to be conformed to the likeness of Christ?*
   - *How do you feel about this destiny?*

---

[2] Genesis 12:3b

- *Will you allow Him to shape you into a vessel that reflects the true image of Christ to the world?*
- *Will you allow Him to cut off everything in you that does not reflect Him?*
- *Will you allow Him to deposit a world-changing beauty in you that draws all men unto Him?*

You must settle these issues in your heart. The Lord predestined you to be conformed to His image, but if your heart is set on a different destiny, you will struggle in frustration your entire life.

Do some honest soul searching and wrestle with the questions. If you can honestly answer yes to them, write out a prayer of surrender and commitment to the Lord. If you can't answer yes, ask the Lord to show you what's in the way and to help you deal with those areas. Write a prayer sharing your struggles, questions, and fears with Him. Then listen and write His response to you.

2. *What uncomfortable or painful treatments are you going through right now? Can you see what the Lord wants to develop in you through them? Can you see His loving commitment to your wholeness? If you can't see or aren't sure, ask Him to show you.*

How are you doing at submitting to His working? Are you moldable clay in His hands? If you have hardened yourself lately, ask His Spirit to soften you that you might be moldable clay once again, ready to respond to His every nudge. He's committed to your wholeness, so you'd better believe He is going to keep working on you until you allow Him to fully prune and refine the areas He is working on. Don't get so caught up in your circumstances that you miss what God wants to do in you through them. Allow the Master to do His life-giving work in you!

FULLY RADIANT

I desire for you to radiate my love and glory.

Radiant with My Love

*"I sought the Lord, and he answered me; he delivered me from all my fears. Those who look to him are **radiant**; their faces are never covered with shame." Psalm 34:4-5*

*"Commit your way to the Lord; trust in him and he will do this: He will make your righteousness **shine like the dawn**, the justice of your cause like the noonday sun." Psalm 37:5-6*

*"And we, who with **unveiled faces all reflect the Lord's glory**, are being transformed into his likeness with **ever-increasing glory**, which comes from the Lord, who is the Spirit."* 2 Corinthians 3:18

"Beloved, I long to lead you deeper and deeper into my presence until you are radiant with my love. Look up, my girl. Take your eyes off of the circumstances around you and look into my glorious face. All it takes for my breathtaking radiance to completely take over your countenance is for you to look at me, to meet with me face to face. The love you will see emanating from my soul through my smile and eyes will immediately bring forth light from your own face, for my radiance and glory are contagious. Truly, my child, as you lift up your eyes from staring at your feet, your mistakes, the people around you, and the circumstances you find yourself in, I will remove all shame from your face and replace it with my radiant glory. For those who look to me are radiant! Not those who work really hard in my name. Not those who try really hard to love others in their own strength. Not those who strive to please me and everyone around them. Not those who cover their faces with make-up. And not those who try to exude a radiance of their own. No, it's *those who look to me* whose faces are radiant.

Allow my love to cast out all your fears, my grace to cast out all your shame, and my delight to cast out all your insecurities. Let my unconditional, overwhelming love penetrate your soul, and you will begin to radiate from the inside out. You see, my love has that effect on people. Beautiful, as you allow me to draw you into the intimate love relationship with me that you were created for, you will radiate with my spirit and love. Human love sometimes has that effect on people. When a young couple falls in love, they often have that "honeymoon glow" about them. But the glow always fades. Human love comes and goes, but my divine love is forever constant, and the subtle glow that stems from human romance is nothing compared to the glorious light that consumes the recipients of my love.

The glow that encapsulated Moses' face after time in my presence is still available for my people today—and to an infinitely greater degree of brightness than Moses experienced. In his second letter to the Corinthians, Paul compared the glory Moses reflected to the glory we should reflect today:

*"If the ministry that condemns men is glorious, **how much more glorious** is the ministry that brings righteousness! For what **was** glorious has no glory now in comparison with the **surpassing glory**. And if what was fading away came with glory, **how much greater** the glory of that which lasts!"*[1]

Oh Beloved, Moses' face shone with my glory from the limited access he had to my presence. He didn't get to enjoy the free, unrestricted access to me that is available for you today. In his

---

[1]   2 Corinthians 3:9-11

day, there was still a curtain in my temple that separated my people from the holy of holies—the place where my manifest presence dwelt. And even those priests who went through all the cleansing rituals and sacrifices to enter that inner sanctuary were only given one-time admittance before having to perform all the ceremonies again.[2] But Beloved, the curtain that separated man from my presence is forever destroyed now. Jesus' death shattered that barrier forever. You now have free, unlimited access to my throne room.[3] It is available at any time, any day, and you can come as close as you want. There is no barrier to the depths of intimacy that we can enjoy together. You are now completely accepted in my presence, fully righteous and innocent before me because you come bearing Christ's innocence and perfection.

Can you see that the radiance which marked Moses' face is nothing compared to the radiance that can now shine forth from yours? His face glowed with limited access to me. How much more will yours shine from your constant, unlimited access to me! Come and know me, Beloved! Come into my chambers, come gaze into my eyes, come listen to my heart, and the light of my love and presence will begin to shine forth from you. Come know how loved you are, come fall in love, and every part of you will begin to glow.

When this happens, the world will come to know me for who I really am. For truly, you will shine as the light of the world.[4] You won't strive to be light—you'll just naturally shine forth my light. It will radiate from within and you won't be able to contain it. Moses didn't try to make his face glow—it was just the natural by-product of time in my presence. Trust me, my girl, as you

---

[2] Leviticus 16:1-34
[3] Hebrews 10:19-23
[4] Matthew 5:14

spend time in my presence, you will shine even greater than he did, and this world will be drawn to the Light of Life. They will be drawn to me!

I am inviting you near. Come into my chambers! Come and know your value and come experience my life-changing love. You and this world will never be the same!"

* Breathing Exercises:

1. *Set aside some time to "look to the Lord" today. Go into your room, sit in your backyard, find a nearby prayer chapel, pull your car off to the side of the road—just find a space where you can seek His face. Quiet your heart and mind and begin to focus your thoughts on the Lord. Take your eyes off the circumstances surrounding you and focus them on your King. Ask to see His face. Ask to see His smile over you and the twinkle in His eyes. Gaze upon His beauty and enjoy Him. Receive His love for you!*

2. *The Lord doesn't make us radiate just for the sake of radiating. He longs for our radiance to draw the world to **Him**! But so often we act like Moses and try to cover our radiance. We keep this incredible love relationship to ourselves and hide it from those around us. Maybe we're embarrassed, maybe we're ashamed, maybe we're scared of what they'll think, or maybe we're just selfish and self-consumed.*

   Moses put a veil over his face after spending time in the Lord's presence in order to keep the Israelites from gazing at the radiance. In what ways do you do the same thing? Do those around you know the reason for the hope that you have and the glow on your face? How can you remove your veil to allow the Lord to shine brightly through you to a lost and hurting world? Let the Lord free you from your embarrassment and fear! Let go of the things you hide behind and let your light shine brightly for all to see. Let them see the beautiful glory of the King and be drawn to Him! Find one tangible way to "remove a veil" this week and to let your light freely and naturally shine for others.

Soaking Time

*"But thanks be to God who always leads us in triumphal procession in Christ and through us spreads everywhere **the fragrance of the knowledge of him**. For we are to God the aroma of Christ among those who are being saved and those who are perishing." 2 Corinthians 2:14-15*

"Before a girl's turn came to go in to King Xerxes, she had to complete twelve months of beauty treatments prescribed for the women, six months with oil of myrrh and six with perfumes and cosmetics." Esther 2:12

"Beloved, I'm calling you to soak in my presence like Esther soaked in her baths of oils and perfumes. I want to make you like her—a dazzling queen, the most beautiful of all the ladies. But this doesn't come from an easy life or getting everything you want when you want it. It comes from beauty treatments, some of which aren't fun. It comes from hours at my feet and in my presence. It comes from regular soaking times.

Esther and the other women contesting to become Queen spent twelve months soaking in baths of oils and perfumes in preparation to meet the King. Twelve months of fragrant baths! This could be seen as a waste of time, but these ladies understood a profound truth about beauty and fragrance. They didn't want fading beauty. They knew that to be fit for the King, beauty and fragrance must become a permanent part of their nature. Instead of spraying on a nice external fragrance in the morning that would fade in a few hours, they wanted that fragrance to become part of them and to flow from every pore in their bodies. They sought to immerse themselves in the fragrance so long that it completely soaked into who they were and became a scent that flowed from the inside out.

Beloved, that's what I want for you. I don't want you to spray a little "God fragrance" on in the morning. I don't want you to merely have an external, fading fragrance for others to smell. I don't want you to put on an external show of love or spirituality. I want it to emit out of the core of who you are. I want you to soak in me until my intoxicating fragrance begins to radiate from the inside out.

So much of your fragrance right now comes from the outside, but I am inviting you to soak in my presence until my nature saturates every part of your spirit and soul. Only then will others be captivated by me and my fragrance. They won't understand what it is that's so intoxicating about that fragrance, but they'll know they have to be near it. They will be drawn to you, and through you I will draw them to myself. Yes, some will be turned off by it, but those who I am drawing to myself won't be able to stay away. They will recognize it as the scent of life that their hearts have always longed for.

So soak in me, my child. Soak in the fragrant, healing, life-giving oil of my Spirit. Surrender to and enjoy these beauty treatments right now. I am depositing something permanent, beautiful and breathtaking in you. Just receive. You don't have to strive. Soak in me and I will begin to fill you with my intoxicating fragrance from the inside out."

* Breathing Exercises:

1. *What type of fragrance do you think you give off to those around you? Is it the life-giving fragrance of Christ? Do*

*you think it draws others to Him? In what ways do you see yourself simply trying to "spray on" a spiritual fragrance to impress people, rather than having it flow from the inside out? Talk through your answers with the Lord and ask Him how He wants you to respond so that His intoxicating nature becomes **your** nature and you authentically spread His fragrance wherever you go.*

2. *Set aside an hour of "soaking time" this week. This can look different for each person. Think about the ways that **you** connect best to the Lord. Here are some ideas:*

   - *Soak in some scriptures about aspects of God's nature that you want Him to develop in you. John 13:1-17 and Philippians 2:5-11 are great passages to soak in. As you read and reflect on these scriptures and soak in the beautiful fragrance of Christ that flows from them, pray for His fragrance to begin to seep into the depths of your own nature and heart.*

   - *Take a walk with the Lord in His creation and soak in His beauty, creativity, and love. Soak in His companionship and presence. Enjoy Him as you walk together.*

   - *Put some worship music on and sing and dance for the Lord! Sing to Him, let Him sing over you, and enjoy His wonderful presence. Soak in His love, goodness, and words to you.*

   - *Find a comfy place in your home or outside to simply "be" with the Lord. Soak in His friendship and presence. Don't feel the need to say anything. Just rest knowing that He's there with you and delights in the quiet time with you. Listen to anything He might say to you, but be content if He just wants to "be" with you.*

- *Go to a prayer chapel, or light candles in your room with soft music to create a "soaking space." Pray, journal, paint, draw, dance, sing, listen, build, rest, or nap in His presence.*

Feel free to try a couple of these ideas throughout this week or month. Invite your friends to "soak" with you. Make "soaking times" a consistent part of your life! Let Him flow through you from the inside out!

PART 2

OVERFLOWING WITH HIS FULLNESS

"Beloved, the promises in Ephesians 3:17-21 contain your inheritance and your destiny. They describe the reality I created you to live in every moment of every day. I invite you to soak in this passage until you begin to live out the fullness of these words."

"I pray that you, being rooted and established in love, may have power, together with all the saints, to grasp how wide and long and high and deep is the love of Christ, and to know this love that surpasses knowledge—that you may be filled to the measure of all the fullness of God. Now to him who is able to do immeasurably more than all we ask or imagine, according to his power that is at work within us, to him be glory in the church and in Christ Jesus throughout all generations, forever and ever! Amen." Ephesians 3:17-21

FULLY ROOTED

"And I pray that you, being rooted and establised in love . . ." Ephesians 3:17

Roots

Paul kneels before the Father and begins his prayer in Ephesians 3:17 by fervently praying that the believers in Ephesus would be rooted and established in God's love. He longs for them to shine as a radiant church overflowing with God's fullness, but he knows that will never be possible if they aren't rooted in the right place. Everything in their lives, church, city, ministry, and relationship with Christ hinges on the depth and placement of their roots. This is the foundation for everything God wants to do in and through them!

Roots serve two main functions for a plant: they are an anchor system and a feeding system. As an anchor system, the roots secure the plant into the ground so that it cannot be moved and ripped up when winds and storms come. The roots make the plant firm and stable in the place it has been planted. The greater the root system, the more secure and unmovable the plant will be.

Roots also serve as a feeding system. They are the vessel through which the plant gets the nutrients it needs to grow, flourish, and produce fruit. It cannot survive without the nutrients of the soil, and it can only receive those nutrients through the roots. They spread out through the soil, find water and food, and then suck up everything the plant needs for growth.

It's a pretty amazing system! But the interesting thing to me is that no one sees the roots, and most people rarely think about them. As I sit here typing in my backyard, gazing at the beautiful rose bush that greets me every morning, I realize that I've never once given a thought to the roots of this plant. When I think about my rose bush, I think of the vibrant pink flowers, the intoxicating fragrance, the healthy leaves, and even the prickly thorns. I don't think about the roots; as the saying goes, "out of sight, out of mind." But the truth is that the vibrancy, sweet aroma, beauty, health, and longevity of this plant all depend on the roots. The splendor of my rosebush is the fruit of a healthy root system planted in the right soil.

I often view my life in the same way I view my rosebush. I focus on all of the surface realities that my physical eyes can see, and I ignore the inner unseen realities of my own heart and the world around me. If I'm stressed at work, I attribute it to the back-log of unopened e-mails on my computer and the long to-do list sitting on my desk. I assume the stress will leave once I get "caught up" on everything. Therefore, I deal with it by taking a few deep breaths and a quick walk around the block to relieve my tension headache and then jump back in to tackle the numerous tasks on my plate. I assume that once I finish I'll be at peace. But that's like looking at one of my wilting roses and assuming that massaging the petals and pouring a little water over them will revive them. We first need to look at what's going on with the roots and the soil they are planted in.

If I'm feeling stressed at work, I'm learning to take a time-out to examine my roots with the Lord. Where am I sending my roots for security and nourishment? Am I dependent on the praise and approval of other people for health? Am I rooted in my own sense of perfectionism and drive to accomplish more and more in order to "be enough"? Am I rooted in the need to perform well? Or am I rooted in God's unconditional love and acceptance of me? Am I rooted in fear or in confidence of God's power and heart for me? Am I more aware of the pressures surrounding me, or God's smile over me? Am I rooted in physical facts or eternal truths? The *fact* might be that I let someone down and didn't finish everything that others were expecting of me, but the *truth* is that God is still smiling over me and His delight, acceptance and love for me have not changed one bit. Which reality am I more aware of and rooted in?

I know that right now much of my identity is rooted in my accomplishments and the praise or approval of others. If I feel like I'm doing a good job and others seem to be admiring me, then I feel stable. But if I feel like I'm not measuring up or others are disappointed with me, I am shaken and insecure. But the thing is, I don't want to be rooted in these places. I long for my roots to be firmly grounded in God's love for me. *Lord, how do I do it? How do I rip up my roots from these other places and send them deep into your love instead?*

"I will teach you, Beloved. It's a journey that requires you to be very intentional. Recognizing the places that you send your roots is the first step. Once you identify the soil that you send them to for stability and nutrients, I will help you to uproot them and move them to the soil of my love instead. I will show you how; just keep following my lead.

My child, in the natural world a healthy root system is often developed through stress and harsh conditions. When a tree receives no water for a while, it sends its roots to look for moisture in deeper places. Good gardeners know this truth and often withhold water at certain times to help the plant develop strong, healthy roots. They know the importance of a healthy root system for the long-term vitality and survival of the tree. It is this practice of allowing "stress" on the plant that will prepare the root system to survive future storms and keep the tree alive and thriving in any weather.

Beloved, I am that skilled and caring gardener. I do allow certain "stresses" to hit you, but only for your good and wholeness—only because I want to see you thrive! You can allow stress and harsh conditions to rip you up from the ground and damage you, or you can allow them to push your roots deeper into my goodness and love, making you strong, healthy, and whole. The choice is yours. Will you choose to see hard circumstances as an opportunity to develop a healthy root system that will allow you to thrive through every season for the rest of your life? This is my heart and intention for you—a life of wholeness, strength, and health for your entire being. See the circumstances surrounding you as the incredible opportunity that they are!"

* Breathing Exercises:

1. *Take some time to look under the surface of your circumstances and heart to see where your roots are searching. Where are you looking for stability and security? Where are you looking for food and fulfillment for your soul? Repent of any place you have sent your roots other than God. Ask Him to uproot you from those areas and to plant you in His life-giving love.*
2. *Make a commitment this week to stop and consider your roots every time you find yourself stressed, fearful, anxious, or frustrated. Take the extra time to look beyond the surface of things to see the placement of your roots and how that placement is affecting your emotions. Deal with the root issue once you identify it with God. Ask Him to help you get rooted in His love instead. Then enjoy the freedom that comes from moving your roots to the right place!*

Rooted by the Stream

*"**Cursed** is the one who **trusts in man**, who depends on flesh for his strength and **whose heart turns away from the Lord**. He will be like a bush in the wastelands; he will not see prosperity when it comes. He will dwell in the parched places of the desert, in a salt land where no one lives.*

*But **blessed** is the man who **trusts in the Lord**, whose **confidence is in him**. He will be like a tree planted by the water **that sends out its roots by the stream**. It does not fear when heat comes; its leaves are always green. It has no worries in a year of drought and never fails to bear fruit."*
Jeremiah 17:5-8

Oh to become like the life-giving tree in this passage—firmly rooted in the ever-flowing stream of God's love, never worrying, and always producing fruit. This is my dream, but so often I live like the bush in the wastelands instead. It amazes me that the only difference between these two plants is the location of their confidence and trust, the location of their roots. One trusts in man and lives a cursed, lonely, empty existence. The other places all his trust in God and enjoys an incredibly abundant, peaceful, fruitful life that brings glory to God and life to others.

May we learn the deep truths found in this picture. If we want to live as the life-giving tree, our confidence can't be in ourselves and our ability to control things or in others and their love and praise for us. Our trust can't be in the things of this world or the circumstances around us. When our trust is placed in anything

141

other than our loving, mighty God, we become that shrub in the desert that lives a barren life and sadly doesn't see prosperity when it comes. In other words, we don't recognize the blessings that God is pouring out on us. We live under a curse.

Cursed seems like a very strong word to me, but I'm learning that this issue of where I send my roots really is an issue of life and death for my soul. Satan tries to disguise it as a minor issue in our lives—low on the totem pole compared with other issues and sins. I've fallen for his trick many times, writing this issue off as having minor importance. *Yeah, I know I shouldn't care so much what others think, but* . . . and I come up with a million reasons why my concern about their opinion is valid and important and why I don't have time to pray and take a good look at the root issue. Or, *Yeah, I know I shouldn't cling to control so much and need to do everything myself, but* . . . and I list off all the reasons why I don't fully trust God or others to come through and why it's much easier just to rely on myself.

But God doesn't cut any corners when He addresses this issue. Anyone who places their trust and confidence in man rather than God lives under a curse. This means that people who spend the day trying to gain the approval of others, who depend on their own success to fulfill them, and who look to others or themselves to meet their own needs are living cursed. It's not that God curses people who do these things; it's that we send our roots into cursed soil that holds no life or nutrients for us. The ground of "trusting in man" is cursed and will never produce the fruit of joy, peace, and life that we are looking for, yet it is where many of us continue to place our roots, deceived into believing that this soil can produce the security and fruit we're longing for.

I'm so sorry Lord. You've warned me that this soil is cursed, but I haven't believed you or heeded your warning. I think part of me doesn't know how to rip my roots up from this soil. I've been rooted here for so long that I don't seem to know how to send them anywhere else. I think my root system is often split. I send some of them into your love, but then I send others into the approval and love of man. I can get quick nutrients from the soil of man (my own accomplishments, self-righteousness, love from others), but it seems that I have to dig longer and deeper in the soil of your love to find nutrients and security there. It's a harder and longer process to send my roots out "by the stream"—one that takes deliberate intention. And most days I don't feel like I have the time to be that intentional about where I send my roots, so they end up by default in the "trust of man."

*But I don't want to live this way any longer. I'm sick of living under this curse. It truly is a curse—I feel the horrible effects of it every day: stress, anxiety, fear of disappointing others, emptiness, busyness, weariness, disappointment, frustration, and lack of peace. I want to send my roots into the life-giving stream of your love and to live as that vibrant, secure, life-giving tree! Your word says that the only difference between this life-giving tree and the lifeless shrub in the desert is the placement of their trust. I **must** choose to place all of my trust and confidence in you. And in order to do that, I must continue to get to know your heart for me. There's no other option. I've got to continue to meditate on, study, and soak in the truth of your heart towards me so that I can fully pour all of my trust and confidence into you. I want to seek to know your heart with everything in me. There is no greater pursuit. Lord, continue to speak to me and help my entire heart, soul, and mind to become completely rooted in your overflowing love!*

* Breathing Exercises:

1. *In what ways do you find yourself rooted in the cursed soil of "trusting in man"? Who do you tend to trust in and what do you trust them for? Reflect on the consequences*

you experience as a result. In what ways does your life look like the shrub in the wastelands? What makes it hard for you to trust God with these situations instead of man? Ask for His forgiveness and a revelation of His heart and power that you might learn to transfer your trust onto Him. Ask Him to help uproot you from the cursed soil you find yourself in.

2. *Make some changes this week to send your roots into the stream of God's love. There is a life-giving stream available for you, but it's up to you to tap into it. Come up with three tangible steps you can take this week to send your roots into this stream. Here are a few ideas to get you started:*

- *Soak in some good worship music about the love, nature, and heart of God as you wake up, drive to work, head to school, or work around the house.*
- *Spend the first half hour of your day in God's word, getting rooted in the truth of who He is.*
- *Take a 15 minute time-out in the middle of each day to examine where your roots are and who you're trusting in. Are you trusting in man or God? If you find yourself trusting in man in certain areas, go to the Lord in prayer and stay there until you are fully able to release each area to Him in the complete trust and confidence that He will care for you.*

Basking in His Love

If I want my roots to go deep into God's love, I know that basking in Him is one practice that must become part of my daily life. God introduced me to the practice of basking a few years ago through my dear friend, the Butterfly. I have always loved butterflies—there's something about them that makes my heart skip a beat, an involuntary smile spread across my face, and praise to God leap up in my spirit. I'm convinced that God is flirting with me whenever He sends one fluttering by, and I often get butterflies in my own stomach in those moments.

As I've studied these incredible creatures, I've learned about their daily practice of basking. You see, when a butterfly wakes up in the morning, it can't fly. Butterflies are cold-blooded creatures and their bodies are close to air temperature when they are at rest. They can't fly when their temperature is below 60 degrees Fahrenheit, so they must raise their body temperature by basking in the sun each morning: spreading out their wings and collecting energy until their entire body is warm enough to fly. By basking, a butterfly can raise their body temperature 15-20 degrees![1]

The truth is that I'm much like these dear friends of mine. I too take on the temperature of the atmosphere surrounding me. If I'm in a stressed environment, I feel stressed. If the circumstances around me are dark and oppressive, I feel it and

---

[1] Patti and Milt Putnam, *North America's Favorite Butterflies* (Minocqua: Willow Creek Press, 1997), 16.

heaviness rests on me. I'm easily affected by the anger, pain, and disapproval of others. But God desires for me to fly above these circumstances—letting Him alone determine the state of my heart, rather than mirroring my circumstances. He longs to raise the temperature of my peace, joy, contentment, and love far beyond the surroundings I may find myself in.

So, like the butterfly, I need to bask. I'm learning that if I want to be a creature who lives unhindered by the circumstances in which I find myself, who touches lives and reflects the glory of God, then I must bask in His presence each morning. Basking is a time for me to enjoy Him, His love, and His heart. It's not a time to "accomplish" anything or study or write—it's a time just to be with the one who has called me into fellowship with Himself. There are no "shoulds" in this time—nothing I "should" be doing or accomplishing. For a 'doer' like me, this is quite a hard assignment, but it's so necessary.

The results of this type of basking are like those of sunbathing. When you spend time in the sun, it affects your appearance. You don't have to do anything to get tan—all you do is show up and the sun does the rest of the work. The sun's rays are so powerful that they automatically begin to change the pigment of your skin as soon as you expose yourself to them. The same is true with the Lord. All I have to do is hang out in His presence—basking, playing, resting—and His presence begins to change me. Even if I don't think anything is happening, He *is* changing me and the rays of His love begin to beautifully tan places of my heart. When you spend hours in the sun, it automatically shows in your complexion. The same is true with the Lord. It's obvious when you meet people who spend much time basking in the love and presence of their King. Their heart, soul, and even physical bodies radiate a golden glow of confidence, peace, joy, and love that can only come from the throne room. I long to be this type of basker!

One day, the Lord showed me one of the main tactics of the enemy. This has helped me understand how critical basking is. Our adversary's strategy is this:

If I can keep all these Christians busy serving and involved in ceaseless activities, they'll never have time to truly *know* God, be captivated by His love, or enter into the powerful intimacy this whole thing is supposed to be about. They'll never be filled to the measure of all the fullness of God and never be the radiant, world-changing force that they can be. If I can keep them so busy with activity that they don't have time for a relationship with God, I'll keep them forever in a powerless cycle of busyness with no real threat to my work.

Yikes, I've definitely seen the success of this tactic in my own life. But I'm on to him now, and I don't want to allow him this power anymore. I don't want to live a powerless "good" life of service, busyness, and striving. I want to live a passionate, radical life of love, power, and intimacy with the Lord, a life where I radiate His love because I've spent so much time basking in it.

* Breathing Exercise:

1. *Set aside some "basking time" this week. This will look different for each person. The only requirement is that you **enjoy** the Lord during the time. This is not a time to accomplish anything—just a time to **be** with the One who has called you into fellowship with Himself. You could lay out in the sun with Him, go on a walk or bike ride, read an enjoyable book with Him (not something*

*that makes you feel productive though), climb a tree, or any other activity that helps you enjoy Him. Whatever you do, seek to be aware of the God who **is** with you and deeply delights in you. Seek to be still and know that **He** is God. Rest in His presence and His love. Take a break from the frantic "doing" and busyness of your life. Seek to simply be with Him and enjoy Him!*

Established in Love

*"And I pray that you, being rooted and **established in love** . . ."*
Ephesians 3:17b

Paul not only prays for the Ephesians to be rooted in God's love, but to also be *established* in that love. The Greek word here for "established" means to lay a basis for, to lay a foundation for, to ground, and to settle. It's the same word used to describe the wise man in Matthew 7:25 whose house did not fall in the storm because it was "founded" on the rock. God's love has to be the foundation of our lives—the basis for all we think, say, and do. Every other foundation will crumble beneath us. Foundations are crucial, but because our fast-paced society wants quick results and instant gratification, we often zoom past the foundation stage of things. God, however, is not in the same hurry that we are to erect projects, buildings, and seasons in our lives. He is a wise builder who will take as long as necessary to develop a firm foundation for what He's about to do in us and through us.

It amazes me that Jesus didn't enter his public ministry until he was 30 years old and that it only lasted for three years. Three years: that's the snapshot the world received of the God of the universe in the flesh. Why only three years? Why did he wait to start until he was 30 years old? I don't know all the reasons, but I know that during those first 30 years of his life, God was building a crucial foundation for Jesus to stand on, live in, and minister from. Jesus was getting rooted and established in his Father's love, and the future of the world rested on this foundation. If

Christ was not firmly grounded on this unshakable foundation, I don't believe he would have made it through the cross. When all hell broke loose around him, the 30 foundational years of learning his Father's heart and getting firmly grounded in His love was what kept him from being sucked up and washed away by the tsunami of evil and pain that descended upon him. Yes, those 30 years were extremely critical. It was from the relationship and foundation built during those years that Jesus was able to accept the cup the Father gave him in the garden and walk to the cross. For us. Yes, foundations are crucial.

When something is established, there is a history behind it. It's established because it has been tested and proven over and over again. There is a foundation that it has been built upon. Paul prays that we would be established in God's love, grounded in the history of it. God has demonstrated His love, revealed it, and proven it from the beginning of time. It is this foundation that we can stand on. But in order to do that, we've got to know the incredible demonstration of His love woven throughout the pages of Scripture, the stories of people around us, and our own lives. We must learn and study these stories, share our stories with one another, and choose to remember the millions of demonstrations of God's never-ending love. We must follow Jesus' example of getting firmly established on the foundation of God's love so that when the storms come and we don't "feel" his love, we will continue to stand. When Jesus felt completely forsaken on the cross, the only thing he could stand on was the incredible history of His Father's love that had never changed throughout time and surely wouldn't change at that moment.

Lord, help us to become people who are firmly established in Your love. May we be storytellers who continue to remind ourselves and others of your legacy of love. May we testify to your faithfulness in our lives and throughout history and build our faith on these truths rather than the shifting circumstances around us. Make us firm vessels that are unshakably rooted and established in your love!

* Breathing Exercises:

1. *Take some time to write down all the ways God has demonstrated His love in your life. Reflect back over the years, on all the big and small ways He has poured out His faithful love onto you. This history is so important to know, own, and remember. Your testimony is much more than the story of how you met Jesus. Your testimony includes all of the ways God has poured out His lavish and faithful love into your life. Thank Him for these memories and share some of them with at least one person this week. Become a storyteller of the history of God's love!*

2. *Ask a few people this week to share with you one story of God's faithfulness and love in their life. This will help them to get further established in the history of His love as they remember and tell their story, and it will also help build up your foundation!*

FULLY LOVED

"May (you) have power, together with all the saints, to grasp how wide and long and high and deep is the love of Christ." Ephesians 3:18

Further Up and Further In

Stumbling through a wardrobe of old fur coats, four children begin to hear the crunch of new fallen snow beneath their feet and watch in wonder as the coat sleeves brushing against their faces slowly turn to pine branches. Suddenly, they are no longer enclosed in a dark wardrobe, but find themselves surrounded by a beautiful forest, new fallen snow under their feet, and a great expanse in all directions. No longer in England, the children now find themselves in the magical land of Narnia!

If you are familiar with the story, you know the great adventures awaiting them upon their entrance into Narnia. But what if the children had decided to only stay at the entrance of this great land? What if they never ventured past the lone lamp post and immediate trees? What a tragedy it would be. For there are great lands to explore within Narnia, seas to sail, princes to meet, and kingdoms to conquer! They are meant to rule and reign as kings and queens in this great land. This is Aslan's territory and the dimensions, joys, and wonders of his Kingdom are limitless. They would be crazy to stay at the entrance while the Great King calls them to come "further up and further in."[1] Oh, the joys and adventures they would miss out on!

---

[1] C.S. Lewis, *The Last Battle* (New York: HarperCollins Publishers, 1984), 181. These are actually Aslan's words to them in the final Narnia book when he welcomes them into the New Narnia. But I believe this invitation to come further up and further in exists throughout all of the Narnia books.

Yet, sadly, this is where I remain most days: at the entrance of God's love. God invites us to come "further up and further in" to explore the great and glorious expanse of His Kingdom of love, but few of us take Him up on the invitation. We're content to stay right at the entrance of His love, shying away from the adventure He beckons us to. We're content to read a verse about it here and there, sing about it at church, and do the best we can to talk ourselves into believing this divine love is real and life changing. For most of us, His love seems a bit too intangible and elusive to truly grasp, so we quit our pursuit early, convinced that the surface of His love is all that we'll ever understand. We made it to Narnia didn't we? At least we're here in a new Kingdom. Life right here at the entrance will have to do. After all, venturing in further would take courage, time, faith, and effort. It's dangerous and unknown and there isn't a map or step-by-step directions. We have lives to live and things to do, so we settle for this tiny view of the Kingdom.

The early Ephesian believers faced the same temptation, but Paul refused to let them settle for a life lived merely at the entrance of God's love. Getting rooted and established in God's love is important, but it isn't enough. To stop there would be to stop at the entrance of Narnia. They might be rooted in the new reality of God's love, just as the children were rooted in the new reality of Narnia, but getting rooted in that new place isn't all there is—there's so much to explore in that new land! So much further to go!

So Paul prays that after getting rooted and established in God's love, they would be filled with power to be able to grasp the incredible dimensions of that love. The width, length, height, and depth of God's love are endless, rich expanses filled with unthinkable treasure for those willing to explore them. Paul prays that the Ephesian believers won't miss this treasure. He prays for the Lord to fill them with the power they need to collectively embark on this journey and to grasp the unimaginable riches hidden along the way. He prays that they would journey as one body, and that together they would be a people radically transformed by God's love, overflowing with all of His fullness.[2]

This is my prayer as well. I long to journey "further up and further in" that I might grasp the width, length, height, and depth of God's love. *Oh Lord, lead me forward! Teach me how to mine the depths of your love and to grasp their immeasurable dimensions!*

* Breathing Exercises:

1. *If we compare the Kingdom of God's love to the land of Narnia, where are you currently living? Are you vacillating back and forth between the wardrobe and the entrance to Narnia? Are you living right at the entrance, too busy or scared to venture further in? Or are you exploring the dimensions and tasting the wonders of this great land? Spend some time dreaming about where you would like to live and talk to the Lord about those desires.*

2. *Ask the Lord to show you some of the places in this great Kingdom that He would like to take you to. Ask Him to show you the territories He created you to reign in. (Are you destined to rule in the area of peace, taking authority over fear, anxiety, and worry? Or maybe you are called to reign in the area of humility, totally secure in God's love and free from the opinions of others). Will you take Him up on this adventure and follow His lead? If your heart is reluctant to venture in, ask Him to help you identify the reasons and to bring healing into those areas so that you can move on into the adventure He created you for.*

---

[2] Ephesians 3:18-19

Grasping

The Greek word used in Ephesians 3:18 for grasp is "katalambano," which means to take eagerly, seize, possess, apprehend, attain, comprehend, find, obtain, and perceive. It is definitely an action verb! When I hear the word grasp, I think of reaching for something, wrapping my grip around it, struggling until I get a firm hold of it, and then clinging to it. There is often desperation in grasping. This isn't a gentle concept like "clasp" or "hold on to." I think of Jack grasping Roses' hand in the icy waters surrounding the sinking Titanic. He was grasping for her and grasping for life. Grasping is not a passive activity—it requires effort and work, strength and heart—and in this case, it also requires the power of God. For it is impossible to grasp the dimensions of God's love without His power and help.

Oh Lord, I want to grasp your love so badly! I'm trying to reach and feel for it, but I'm having trouble wrapping my hands, heart, soul, and mind around it. It's like I get a hold of certain aspects of it, but can't quite get the whole thing. I ask for your mighty power to be able to grasp it. I want to seize it in its entirety, capture it, and cling to it with all that I am. I want to own it for myself—not just believing that it's mine, but actually taking full possession of it.

"Beloved, as you spend time with me and grow in your knowledge of my heart, your capacity to grasp my love will deepen and increase. The truth is that my love for you is so immense that you'll never be able to fully grasp it, but as you walk with me and grow in intimacy with me, you will slowly get a firmer and firmer hold on it. Get rooted and established in my love, seek to know my heart for you, and allow me to fill you with my Spirit and power. As you do, I will help you grasp the dimensions of my love."

Lord, I feel like a little child trying to grasp a great big ball that my tiny hands can't wrap around. My hands can't grasp it, but yours can, and so I ask for your power to come alongside me to help me grasp it!

"Beloved, no prayer could delight my heart more. I long for you to grasp my love even more than you do. For this is what I created you for—a love relationship with me that's real and tangible, so much more than mere theology. I created you to experience my love, and I will help you grasp it. But I need you to pour everything into this pursuit. Seek me and my heart with all that you are. Reach for this understanding of my love, cry out for it, and ask for revelation from me. So many people never fully grasp the magnitude of my love because they are simultaneously grasping for so many other things. Grasp for this, Beloved. Grasp for this understanding of my love and the other things you grasp for won't matter anymore. For once you get it, it will change everything. And as you throw yourself into this pursuit, I will grow your little hands and the extent of their reach. I will fill you with the power and strength that you need."

* Breathing Exercises:

1. *How do you feel about making this your whole-hearted pursuit right now? Does it seem scary? Hard? Exciting? Selfish? Maybe even narcissistic? Talk to the Lord about your emotions and thoughts and ask for His perspective.*

(For me, this pursuit seemed a little selfish at first. After all, shouldn't my one pursuit be to expand God's Kingdom, or bring Him glory, or lead others into a relationship with Him? Those are great pursuits, but none of them are possible without this revelation of the depths of God's love. God cares more about you and I getting this revelation and walking in His fullness than any "work" we can do for Him. For this world and God's Kingdom don't need people trying to work harder for God or striving under the pressure to evangelize more. We simply need more people walking in a revelation of the fullness of His love for them. For when believers walk in this fullness, others will see God for who He really is and seek Him. His love will overflow out of us to transform the world.)

2. *What would it look like to throw yourself into this one pursuit? To let go of everything else you grasp for and to grasp for a revelation of God's love alone? Are you willing to do that? If so, ask the Lord to help you answer these questions:*

    a. *What other things do you need to let go of?*
    b. *What next steps do you need to take? Write down three tangible steps you can commit to doing this week to start this wholehearted pursuit.*

Staggering Dimensions

*"May (you) have power, together with all the saints, to grasp **how wide and long and high and deep is the love of Christ**."*
Ephesians 3:18

How wide is your love Lord?

"It's wide enough to encompass every part of you and then some. I love *all* of you. I love *you*, not just the image you portray to others. I love the real you—the one hidden behind the mask that others have grown to love. My love is wide enough to stretch beyond your sins, weaknesses, and mistakes. No matter how wide your failures stretch, my love stretches wider to cover them. It does not fall short. My love is wide enough for you to be my favorite, along with every other child of mine. It's that big."

How long is your love Lord?

"My love began before the foundations of the world and will last farther into eternity than your mind can fathom. I chose you before the creation of the world to be holy and blameless in my sight[1]—I chose you for intimacy! I predestined you in love to be adopted as my precious child.[2] I had you in mind when I formed the world, and I loved you. Just the thought of you captured my heart before I even formed you. The thought of whom you would be brought a smile to my face—and still does. From the

---

[1] Ephesians 1:4
[2] Ephesians 1:5

beginning of time, I have loved you with an everlasting love, and my love for you will continue for all eternity! Nothing you can do can make me stop loving you this deeply and passionately. My love is truly never-ending. You cannot lose it. I will never remove it from you. I will never stop loving you as passionately as I do right now. You are secure in my love and you get to enjoy it forever. Oh, how I wish you would enjoy it now! Oh, how I wish you would find your security in it and let it cast out your fears and insecurities forever. It is constant no matter what and nothing will be able to separate you from it![3] It is the one sure thing you can count on forever."

How high is your love Lord?

"My love is much higher than any human love you know. It is on a completely different plane. It is not finicky or changeable. It is the highest form of love any person can receive. It is 100% unconditional, true, pure, noble, honest, genuine, and complete. It cannot be earned or lost, and nothing about it is based on the actions of the recipient. It is a love that flows freely and passionately from the One who *is* love. It is the highest caliber of love one can receive, and I am pouring it out on you with extravagant abundance—receive it, enjoy it, and remain in it! When you do, it will raise you to a whole new level of living. It makes royalty out of its recipients and raises them to heights of living and loving that they never knew existed. This height is where I want to take you! You really will soar on wings like eagles."[4]

How deep is your love Lord?

---

[3] Romans 8:39
[4] Isaiah 40:31

"My love is deeper than anything you can imagine! Deep enough to penetrate even your deep-rooted insecurities, wounds, and fears. Deep enough to send me through more suffering and anguish than you can imagine. It is not just an intellectual love from my mind. I love you from the deepest place in me; from the core of who I am. I am love. My love for you is deeper than anything else that is true in this world. It is deeper and truer than your circumstances. It is deeper than anything else on this earth or the one to come. It is ultimate truth. For *I am* the deepest, truest reality in existence, and I am love. The love that burns in me for you is all encompassing, all consuming, overwhelming, zealous, fiery, jealous, and passionate. It flows from the deepest part of me and beats in every fiber of my being. I am consumed with love for you. You have captured my heart in a way that you will never fully understand on earth. You are my delight, my treasure, my joy, my desire, and my Beloved. I created you in such intimate, tender, passionate love, and I created you for love. This is the whole purpose of your existence—an intimate love relationship with me. I created you for a love relationship with me that makes you whole and complete and brings me glory and praise.

My desire is that, through our love and intimacy, others will also be drawn into the love relationship for which I created *them*. I long for intimacy with you and with this world—for all of you to know my glorious love and to share in it with me. I love you with all that I am, and oh, how I long for you to receive that love and then to love me back with all that you are. I burn with love for you and for this world. I could not contain it in heaven and had to come down to earth to pour it out in all its fullness. I love you so much that I would do anything to be near you and for you to draw near to me. My death on the cross was the only way to make that possible. So, I went to the cross to open the door for intimacy with you—to make it possible to be near you—and not just near you but *in* you! That is how deep my love is. Breathe it in, receive it, and remain in it. It will change everything!"

* Breathing Exercise:

1. *Take some time to cry out for your own revelation of the dimensions of God's love for you. These are the words He spoke to me, but the scope of His love is endless, so this is far from the complete picture. Ask Him how wide, how long, how high, and how deep His love is for you. Believe that He wants to answer these questions and write down everything you hear His Spirit speaking. Then soak in His words to you and let them penetrate deep into your heart, mind, and soul.*

FULL REVELATION

"And to know this love that surpasses knowledge . . ."

Ephesians 3:19

Ginosko Knowing

The word Paul uses in Ephesians 3:19 for "know" is "ginosko," which means to be aware of, feel, have knowledge of, perceive, understand, be able to speak about, and be sure of. It is much deeper than possessing knowledge *about* something. Ginosko means to *personally* know someone or something in its entirety. "It is a full participation in the truth or reality being explored. It is the difference between saying "I love you" to a spouse and actually making love."[1] Paul wasn't crying out on his knees for the Ephesians to know *about* God's love. No, he longed for them to *participate* in it and *experience* it: to feel it, enjoy it, be sure of it, and to be so overwhelmed by it that they couldn't stop talking about it.

Ginosko is the same word that Jesus uses in Matthew 7:23 when He says that He will look at some on the day of judgment and tell them plainly, "I never *knew* you. Away from me, you evildoers!" This is a curious statement; for Jesus obviously knew who they were, their names, and every detail of their lives. They may have prophesied in His name and performed many miracles, but they had never entered into a close, personal relationship with Him. They didn't "ginosko" Him.

Ginosko is also the word that the gospel writers use in telling the story about the healing of the woman who had been bleeding

---

[1] Ruth Haley Barton, Invitation to Solitude and Silence: Experiencing God's Transforming Presence (Downers Grove: Intervarsity Press, 2004), 111.

for twelve years. Mark 5:29 says that when she touched Jesus' cloak, she "felt" in her body that she was healed of her affliction. Luke 8:46 states that at the same moment Jesus "perceived" that power had gone out of Him. Both "felt" and "perceived" are the Greek word ginosko. The woman didn't just know intellectually that she was healed—she *felt* it. Her whole body experienced it and was aware of it. Likewise, Jesus didn't just mentally know that power had gone of Him—He felt it and perceived it in His whole being.

This is the kind of "knowing" that Paul prays for. This is the kind of "knowing" that I long for. I don't want to simply know *about* God's love. I don't want it to only be a head-thing for me. I want to feel it like the woman felt her healing. I want to experience it like Jesus experienced power flow from His body. I want to know it personally to the point where it becomes the biggest reality I live in and I can't stop talking about it or smiling because of it.

So Lord, how do we get there? How do I come into an experiential, ginosko knowing of your love that is eminently greater than any human mind can fathom or experience? I know that its bounds are limitless, but I want to plunge into them. Teach me how!

"Beloved, my heart desires for you to know this love in every fiber of your being. I want it to be the biggest reality you live in. This is the kind of love that makes you glow, radiate, and smile all day. It is so unexpected, undeserved, and extravagant. It's the kind of love that can put you on a cloud all day. It's the kind of love that keeps you smiling in the face of trials and impossible situations because you know that my love for you is a stronger force than those circumstances and that I am going to turn them together for your good.

Here's what I want you to do right now: I want you to stop what you're doing every half hour today for about ten seconds and listen to me whisper, "I love you." I'll be speaking these words to you the whole day. I'll be speaking them in your spirit, in your mind, in the sunrise, in the butterfly that passes you, in the cup of tea I provide, in the song on the radio—I'll be speaking them to you just like I do every day. Because I can't help but declare my love to you throughout the day. I want you to get it and receive it today. I want you to ginosko it. So I will tell you and tell you and tell you, and then I'll show you and show you and show you. I love *you* and I deeply desire for you to receive a revelation of this love. More than your service, ministry, fasting, prayer, or any other spiritual discipline, I want you to simply ginosko my love for you. So as I speak my words of love to you today, and as you begin to hear them, please *listen!* Don't just hear the words, but *listen* to them. Let them sink down into your mind and heart and soul. Remain in them for a minute. Believe them. Trust them. And then continue what you're doing. It's going to start changing everything."

* Breathing Exercise:

1. *Follow the Lord's instructions found in the above paragraph. Try to enter into this practice every day this week. See if it begins to make a difference in your heart, mind, and life.*

The Choice

"Beloved, your own belief and trust in my words to you is crucial to coming into a ginosko knowing of my love. It is very possible to hear me say that I love you, but not believe it. You can possess a head-knowledge of my love that your heart doesn't know or trust at the deepest level. But today, I'm inviting your heart and soul to hear and believe everything I mean when I say, "Beloved, I love you and I am *for* you. And my love for you is unconditional—completely independent from anything you do or don't do. I love you just because you're my beautiful creation and child."

Sometimes believing is a choice. A choice you make even when you don't "feel" like it's true, or circumstances don't seem to confirm its truth. Sometimes it's the choice to believe someone's words over what you feel, because you trust that person and know they wouldn't lie to you."

As I listened to the Lord, His words reminded me of the day I had my wisdom teeth removed as a sophomore in college. My mom drove me home from the dentist with specific instructions to remove and replace the gauze in my mouth every hour for the next 24 hours. After the first hour passed, she dutifully knelt to where I was laying on the couch to help replace the gauze. After pulling the pieces out, she started making new wads to put back into my mouth.

"Wait, Mom," I awkwardly mumbled, "you forgot one." I had felt another foreign object in my mouth and was holding it between my fingers.

"Kierra," she said as she tried to suppress a smile, "you're holding your lip."

"No I'm not Mom. I'm not talking about my lip, I'm talking about THIS," as I tried to emphasize what my fingers were holding.

"Kierra, I'm telling you, you are holding your LIP."

"No way," I insisted for I knew there was no way that what I was holding could be my lip. It was a big and foreign object and I would definitely know if it was my lip.

Realizing I wouldn't be persuaded easily, she got up and returned to the couch with a mirror in her hands. "Here," she said with a knowing smile, "take a look for yourself."

I looked into the mirror and couldn't believe what I saw. She was right, I *was* holding my lip. How was that possible? It didn't feel like my lip at all. I was stunned and just kept staring at it. Then giggling, I sheepishly apologized for my lack of trust in her words.

Why did I trust my own perception and feelings over my mom's words? Obviously she could see better than I could and she certainly wouldn't lie to me. But it was so hard for me to believe her when what she *said* totally contradicted what I *felt*. I realized in a new way that my feelings are not always accurate sources of reality. They often mislead me—some days due to large doses of Novocain and other days due to my sinful nature, the culture around me, the enemy, pride, and a variety of other reasons. But God will never mislead me. His words are always truth. He will never lie to me, and He can see much more clearly than I can. His words are always a reliable source for true reality and are always true above my feelings and my own logic. God taught me much about this truth through my 7-year-old friend, Trevor. His aunt found him crying at the top of the steps one day and asked what was wrong.

"My mom only loves me 30%," he sobbed.

"What do you mean?" his aunt asked.

"She loves my sister Kacey 90%, but she only loves me 30%."

"How do you know this?" his aunt inquired.

"Because she always gives me time-outs and I'm always getting in trouble," he sniffed.

"Trevor, I know your mom very well and I know that she doesn't love Kacey more than you. She loves both of you 100%. Just because she has to discipline you when you don't listen to her, it doesn't mean that she loves you less," his aunt reassured him.

But Trevor would not be reassured that day. It didn't matter how much his aunt, or even his mom expressed the truth of her love for him—his own logic and feelings convinced him that his mom only loved him 30%. In his 7-year-old logic, receiving more time-outs than Kacey definitely meant that his mom loved him less.

But the truth is that his mom loves him dearly. She loves him just as much as his sister. She disciplines him when he doesn't listen to her, but only because she *does* love him and wants the best for him.

I can be a lot like Trevor. Sometimes God says things that don't make sense to me. My own logic seems so right to me and I choose to believe my own knowledge over what He says. But God wants to bring me into a knowing of His love that surpasses my knowledge and the things I think I know so well. My own logic *will* conflict with His truth at times, but it is in these times that I must make a choice to believe His words over my own limited knowledge.

* Breathing Exercises:

1. *What is something that God has said to you that doesn't "feel" or "seem" true right now? Think about His words and think about your feelings. Which one is actually truth? Decide to choose His words. Declare their truth out loud and verbally call out and rebuke the lies from the enemy. This is warfare! The fullness of God is definitely something worth fighting for, so give the enemy a run for his money today. It doesn't matter if your feelings don't change instantly. The important thing is that you make a decision to fight for the truth. As you do, your feelings will eventually catch up with true reality and you **will** enter into a* ginosko *knowing of God's love.*

2. *Tell a trusted friend about the truth you are struggling to believe, and the choice you have made to believe God's words over your feelings or logic. Ask them if they would enter this fight with you by speaking truth from His Word over you every day this week. It can be a quick 30-second phone call each day where they simply read and declare His truth to you.*

Receive

I am currently enrolled in massage school, and while I'm gaining skills in releasing knots and tension in people's bodies through my classes, I'm also learning much about the mystery of receiving God's love . . .

It was mid-term day and I couldn't wait to give my first complete 60-minute, full-body massage to my assigned T.A. I wasn't concerned about her evaluation or my grade—I just wanted to love this daughter of God with all my heart. I deeply desired for her to supernaturally feel the love of God through my touch. I prayed for her as I drove to class, I had friends praying back in their homes, and I prayed with all my heart as I lovingly worked on her for that sacred hour. Though I didn't know anything about who she was, her past, or how often she felt loved, I prayed that somehow during that hour, she would feel, maybe for the first time, the love and touch of her Creator.

After the massage, I excitedly followed her into the office where she would give me my evaluation. But all the excitement and joy drained out of my body as she coldly stated, "It was ok," with a dissatisfied look on her face.

"Just ok?" I asked.

"Yes," she replied with little emotion. "You did well on most of it, but you forgot one of the moves on the neck and you left my arms outside the sheet after working on them, so I got cold."

And that was it. She added up my less than perfect score, handed me my paper, and left without even saying thank you.

I was bummed. After all the prayer and love I poured out for her, she totally missed it and walked away seemingly unaffected. Yet God began to reveal some deep truths to me through this experience on my drive home. Here is the entry I wrote in my journal that night:

Oct 20th: Receiving God's love

I'm so frustrated tonight. For an entire hour I prayed over my "client," praying that she would feel loved and cared for by the Spirit of God flowing through me. I touched her with as much love as I knew how; I so badly wanted her to receive the love I was giving her. But she totally missed it. She was so caught up in the logistics of the massage, that she totally missed the touch of love. Her heart and mind were preoccupied and she wasn't ready to receive love.

God, how many times do I fall into bed at night and you feel the same frustration at another day gone by of loving me while I am so preoccupied with other things that I totally miss it? I don't want to miss it anymore. I want to be more preoccupied with receiving your love than any other detail or logistic of the day. I want to feel and experience every ounce of love that you're pouring out on me. I want to receive your love—for that is more important than anything else. Only then will I be secure in you, know who I am, and be filled to the measure of all Your fullness. This has to be my focus and priority for each day. So let's start with today. I know I'm already trying to plan my schedule, but I will let all those details go right now and say that whatever you have planned, I just want to experience your love for me in it. I want to receive every love gift you are giving me, hear every whisper of love you're

*speaking, and feel every touch of love you're bestowing on me.
I want to see the love in your eyes, the delight in your smile,
and the unconditional acceptance in your heart. This matters
so much more than what I accomplish, what I look like, and
what others think of me.*

Another thing I've learned from massage class is that I can't
give something I haven't received. I can't give a good massage
if I haven't received one myself and know from experience
what feels best. The best training I get in my classes is actually
receiving a massage by one of our instructors. As I feel him
work the knots out of my back, I learn what feels best and how
to then provide the same therapy for someone else. I learn far
more about how to give a good massage by receiving one than
by watching one or reading a text book. It's the same in life. I
can't give love to others that I haven't first received from God. If
I want to love others well, the best training I can get is to allow
myself to fully enjoy and receive God's love for me. Receiving
His love is far more powerful than reading about it or watching
others love. *Oh Lord, please teach me to get on your massage
table and allow myself to receive!*

"Beloved, all you need to do is lay down. You don't strive to feel
loved by someone. You just need to be open to it. Let yourself
enjoy and notice my love. Don't be too busy to enjoy it. Don't
be so preoccupied that you miss it. Just keep your heart open
and expectant and attentive throughout the day; keep your
eyes locked on mine and you will know my love. Look for it
and listen to me—I'm whispering words of love, but your own
thoughts are so loud that they often keep you from hearing what
I'm saying. Leave time for romance, deep talks, and quality time.
You'll never fall madly in love in a day of crazy busyness and
preoccupation. Walk through your day in a posture of reception
and I will fill you with more love than you know what to do
with."

* Breathing Exercises:

1. *Can you relate to the T.A. on my massage table, too preoccupied with logistics and other things to allow herself to notice and receive a touch of love from her Creator? What is it that keeps you from receiving His love? What are you preoccupied with? Talk to the Lord about these distractions and listen for His guidance as to how to move past them so you can receive His love today.*

2. *What would it look like for you to walk through your day in a posture of reception, ready for God to fill you with more love than you know what to do with? Let your imagination dream with the Lord as you picture such a day. Then brainstorm a couple steps you can take today to make that dream your actual experience. For it wasn't meant to merely be a nice dream; it was meant to be your daily reality!*

Revelation

"I keep asking that the God of our Lord Jesus Christ, the glorious Father, may give you the Spirit of wisdom and revelation, so that you may know him better." Ephesians 1:17

Lord, I will do my best to listen to your words, believe them, and allow myself to receive your love throughout the day, but I know that much of this ginosko knowing comes from you. I need your supernatural Spirit of wisdom and revelation to help me know you better. So I come to you and I ask for that. I ask for a radical revelation of your love for me and for this world. I ask for a revelation in my spirit—a revelation that undoes me forever. A revelation that leaves me breathless, speechless, and motionless.

My King, please awaken my heart to your love throughout the day. Right now it's awake to so many other things besides your love. It's awake to the guy potentials around me, the opinions of others, the things I don't have, and all the expectations I feel tugging on me for the day. But Lord, instead of these things, I want my heart to be awake to your love. I want your love to be the biggest reality I'm aware of during the day. Please awaken my heart to you!

"Beloved, I will answer this request, but I will do it through giving you a revelation of *me*. This is what you truly need, for as you get a revelation of who I am, you will simultaneously receive a revelation of my love. For I AM love. One of the reasons you have trouble understanding my love is that you keep trying to compare it to earthly, human love. You take the best things you know about human love and try to multiply those qualities by 1,000. But my love is so distinct and completely different than human love. Multiplying the best human love you know by 1,000 will never begin to give you an accurate description of my love. It is a start, but a very, very small start. For though man was made in my image, I am very different from man. I am wholly divine, perfect, good, holy, and I AM true love.

Let me start by giving you a further revelation of who I am. Beloved, I am in control. I reign on high. I am complete and have no need of anything. I am the beginning and the end. I am All in All. I am Life. I am free and I give freedom. I am a joyful dad. I'm a laugher, a dancer, a singer, a giver, a forgiver, and at the core of all of this, I am a lover! It brings me such joy to love you. You're safe in my love, secure in it, free in it, accepted, delighted in, and rejoiced over. Every action I have ever and will ever take is out of love. You are an expression of my love. Every child born is an expression of my love. Every flower, animal, river, and rainbow is an expression of my love. You are surrounded by my love on all sides. Whether you realize it or not, it hems you in behind and before and on every side of you. Because I hem you in and *I AM* love,[1] you are forever covered and protected in perfect love. You are saturated in love. You are surrounded by love much like you are surrounded by air—whether you realize it or not. The core of your identity is that you are a much loved child of God. This is who you are. Rest in it. You're enough. You are loved and you are safe."

* Breathing Exercises:

1. *The words above are the words that the Lord spoke to me as I asked for a deeper revelation of His love and took*

---

[1] Psalm 139:5, 1 John 4:16b

the time to quiet my heart to receive from Him. They are far from a full revelation; they are simply where He chose to start with me this day. I will ask many more times for revelation and I'm sure He will share many more things with me. But now it's your turn. Though I believe these words are true for you, I encourage you to ask for your own revelation from Him. It will be unique in the way He shares it with you. Block off some time and ask Him for a spirit of wisdom and revelation to understand His love at a deeper level. Then wait in expectation to receive from Him. He may respond with a picture, or with words in your Spirit, or with a dream, or with an analogy as you walk to work, or through a conversation with a friend. God reveals truth in many ways, so just be expectant, listening, and open!

2. *When God gives you a new revelation about His love, soak in it! Don't just move on quickly or you will miss some of the power of what He's showing you. Talk about it with Him each day, share it with others, journal about it, and think about it throughout your day. Too often we ask God for a revelation about something and then after He gives it, we quickly move on and forget about it the next day. Savor the treasures He is giving you in this revelation. Let them bring you the riches He intends for you to receive through them.*

FULLY FILLED

"That you may be filled to the measure of all the fullness of God." Ephesians 3:19

Filled

This is it, the climax! This is what everything else has been leading up to. This is why Paul has been pleading on his knees for the Ephesians to become rooted and established in God's love and come into an experiential knowledge of it—all for the sake of **fullness**—overflowing, divine fullness!

This is what we were created for, what life in Christ is all about. This is our destiny as children of God. Let me say that again: if you are a child of God, your destiny is fullness—to be filled to the measure with all the fullness of God. Now *that* is a destiny worth getting excited about!

The Greek word Paul uses in this verse for "filled" is "peleroo" and it means to cram (a net), level up (a hollow), furnish, satisfy, complete, fill up, perfect, and supply. I love these verbs and the incredible picture of fullness that they paint. Let's explore them a little further:

> **To cram a net:** I picture the story in Luke 5:1-11 where the disciples pull up empty fishing nets throw after throw during a fruitless night of fishing. And then I picture those same nets only hours later filled to the breaking point after the disciples obeyed Jesus' instructions to cast them out into the water one more time. Jesus didn't stop at giving them what would be a normal catch, or even a really good catch. He went way beyond what they would ever dream or imagine. He crammed so many fish into those nets that the disciples couldn't even

pull them in; the nets began to break, and their boats began to sink! Now that's what I call fishing, and that's what I call filling! Can you imagine bursting at the seams with God's Spirit and presence, and sinking under the glorious weight of it all? That's His desire for you!

To level up a hollow: A hollow is a hole, a deep hole. To level a hollow is to fill it to the point where there is no hole left, where the chasm is gone. I know hollows; I know voids; I know holes. I think of the deep hollows of my soul, the bottomless chasms, the voids and emptiness that I long to be filled. And I find hope in the promise that when Christ fills us, He will level those hollows until they are completely gone!

To furnish: I think of a family moving into a new home and transforming an empty, bare space into a warm and welcoming home, filling the bare rooms with homey furnishings and touches of love. The filling here isn't so much about quantity as quality. It is the way the filling transforms the whole nature of a place. It is the atmosphere of love, warmth, and invitation that the filling brings. A cold, bare, dark room can be transformed into a bright, life-giving place of warmth with just a few furnishings. The filling changes the nature of the place!

To satisfy: It's been a long day of snowboarding and I arrive home wet, tired, and hungry. After a hot shower, the one thing I want is a warm bread bowl filled with steaming chili. It satisfies the hunger and chill in that moment like nothing else. Mmmm . . . it makes me smile with contentment just thinking about it. To "satisfy" is to do more than to simply meet a need. A peanut butter sandwich could fill my hunger and a cup of hot water could eliminate the inner chill. But those things wouldn't truly satisfy. Satisfaction goes beyond merely meeting a need; satisfaction happens when the filling you receive brings contentment, pleasure, delight, and joy as well. This is the type of filling God brings. His filling satisfies!

To complete: My family members are the champions of Christmas jigsaw puzzles. Every year we kick off the season by pulling out the infamous thousand-piece Santa puzzle, and so begins countless hours of family fun and conversation as we work together to complete the picture. What is it that makes puzzles so addicting? Suddenly I, the girl with the 10pm bedtime, am still hovering over the table at 1am saying, "Just one more piece. I just have to get one more piece in and then I'll head to bed." There's something addicting about finding a place for each of those tiny pieces—something therapeutic about ordering the chaos to come together to make a complete and beautiful picture. Something feels so good about seeing every hole filled and Santa transformed into a complete figure on the table. It's so *fulfilling*! Everyone in my family wants to be present when we put the final piece in. No one wants to miss that moment of triumph and fulfillment as the picture finally becomes whole and complete. No more holes, no more chaotic mess of pieces, just a *complete* and beautiful picture. So Christ's filling *completes* us; He fills in every hole and expertly creates a beautiful picture from the chaos in our lives. And then He shares the joy and satisfaction of this completion with us!

To fill up: I think of my stop on the way to work this morning at the local Chevron Station. With my gas gauge on empty, I knew my Honda wouldn't make it any further without filling up on fuel. It didn't matter how hard he wanted to get me to work (yes, my car is a "he"); it's impossible for him to run on empty. Deep down, I know my heart and soul are the same way. But the good news is that Christ fills me up with everything I need to run strong and thrive throughout the day. There's no running dry or burning-out with Him filling me up!

To Perfect: I picture an artist putting the final touches on her painting. She fills in all the gaps with texture, shading, and intricate details that make the picture come to life. Last week she finished the figures of the grandpa and grandson fishing on a lake, but now it's time to perfect them. Now the painter fills in the shading on their faces, the wrinkles around the grandfather's eyes, and the twinkle inside the boy's. As she perfects the picture, onlookers can now see the deep love in the grandfather's face and the joy and excitement in the boy's. The painter fills in the final reflections off the lake, shadows on the trees, and sun strokes across the sky. And voila! Her masterpiece is now complete and perfect, just the way she pictured it in her head before she made the first stroke across the canvas.

I find so much comfort and joy in this depiction. As the Lord fills me, He perfects me. He fills in every detail and takes great pains to make me just right—the way He pictured me in His mind before I was born. He fills me with everything missing in my character and everything from His nature that I still lack—all my gaps and weaknesses. He perfects me into the beautiful masterpiece that He created me to be, and brings my true identity to life!

To Supply: I think of the way I pack supplies before heading out on a back-packing trip. I will never make it on the journey without ample food, water, and supplies to sustain me along the way. The supplies are a necessity for a fun and successful journey. In a similar way, God promises to supply all our needs on this fun and strenuous adventure with Him through life.[1] As He fills us, He supplies us with everything we need for the journey.

The combination of these verbs creates the complete picture of the filling that God promises. This is what He is all about. He is in the filling business—and not just filling to the bare minimum—He's about filling to the max and then some! The Bible is packed with verses describing His desire to fill His people. He longs to fill us with so much: His joy[2], gladness[3], hope[4], peace[5], wholeness[6], strength[7], presence[8], and so much more. He wants to fill us with everything He is—His very being! Our God wants us full—filled to the measure of all His fullness!

* Breathing Exercises:

1. *Look back through the different verbs used to describe the type of filling that God gives us. Which one do you most desire right now? Take some time to picture what that type of filling would look like in your life. Share your desire with the Lord and ask Him to let you experience that type of filling in the next week. Then be looking for*

---

[1] Philippians 4:19
[2] John 15:11
[3] Psalm 16:11
[4] Romans 15:13
[5] Romans 15:13
[6] Colossians 2:10
[7] Colossians 1:11
[8] Ephesians 1:23

the ways that He begins to answer this prayer. Take the time to notice and thank Him every time He answers your prayer this week! The more you thank Him, the more you will begin to notice and experience new moments of His 'filling.'

2. *Ask the Lord to show you one step you can take this week to help you experience His filling in the way you desire. Ask what your part is. Here are a few examples:*

- ***To cram a net:*** *Your part may be to obey God's instructions to you this day, just as the disciples obeyed and threw their nets in the water again to receive His filling.*
- ***To satisfy:*** *Your part may be to eat the satisfying meal God puts before you. He has set before you a banqueting table, but it's up to you to eat!*
- ***To fill up:*** *You may need to take the time to stop by God's "Filling Station" and ask for the fuel you need, letting Him fill you up.*

*Figure out one step you want to take this week and then do it. The Lord will be faithful to His part and He **will** fill you!*

Flooded with God Himself

"That you may be filled [through all your being] unto all the fullness of God [may have the richest measure of the divine Presence, and become a body wholly filled and flooded with God Himself]!" Ephesians 3:19b Amplified Bible.

I love how the Amplified Bible records Ephesians 3:19. Oh, the joy and wonder of becoming a body wholly filled and flooded with God Himself! To be filled with the richest measure of the divine presence! Can you imagine that? For me, it's a little hard to imagine and believe. It seems too good to be true to think that God's very presence could permanently flood my entire body, mind, and soul—that I could be wholly filled with Him alone. Most days I'm filled to the measure with so many other things: worries, anxieties about my to-do-list, thoughts about myself, preoccupation with my problems and circumstances, and all sorts of other distractions. But God desires to come in and to flood all those things out as He fills me with Himself instead!

I love the word "flooded" in this verse. There's no controlling or stopping a flood—it just takes over. It's disruptive and forceful and leaves a powerful wake of disordered homes and belongings. There's no confusion as to which homes a flood has recently swept through—they are obviously saturated and overflowing with water, and life cannot go on as usual.

Oh Lord, I long for my heart and body to be flooded by you. I yearn for a tidal wave of your divine Presence to come pouring through my entire being and to wash away all this clutter, disrupting the neatly ordered idols in my heart. I want you to fill up every part of me so that I'm overflowing with you and your nature alone. I don't want to be filled with anything else. I long to joyfully overflow with you and your fullness, giving the world an accurate reflection of who you truly are. And I long to see the Church, your Bride, flooded with your presence and powerfully overflowing your fullness into a hurting world.

Wow Lord, what would happen in our world if your people stepped into this destiny? What would happen if all nations, religions, and people groups came into contact with Believers who were filled to the measure with your fullness and presence instead of religion, rules, judgment, self-centeredness, greed, or pride? I think radical things would start happening around the world. I think hungry and thirsty people would come running to find this same fullness for themselves. I think we would actually see your Kingdom come on earth as it is in Heaven. Lord, let it start with me. Let it start with each person reading this book. And then let your fullness overflow out of us onto every person in our lives, and continue to flood through our neighborhoods, cities, nation, and world! This is my heart's cry Father.

"Beloved, this is my heart's cry as well. The desire of my heart is for you and every child of mine to become vessels wholly flooded with my very presence. I want to fill you so completely with myself that you start bubbling over with everything that overflows out of me. I want to fill every nook and cranny of your being with myself and all of my goodness. Your destiny is to be a vessel overflowing with my joy, love, peace, power, compassion, strength, wisdom, goodness, and heart. Beloved, I want you full; I want you overflowing; I want you spilling over with *me*. I want to give you my Spirit without limit![1] I am not

---

[1] John 3:34

a God of small amounts, stingy giving, half measures, meager portions, bare minimums, or little bits. When I say I want to give you my very Self, I don't want to give you a small measure of it—I want you to experience it in all its fullness! I want you spilling over with more abundance than you have ever dreamed or imagined possible.

I desire to give you so much of myself that there's no way you can contain it—it just spills out onto everyone around you. Many will look at your fullness and recognize their own emptiness for the first time. They will ask you where your fullness comes from and you will introduce them to me. Most people have such a distorted image of me. But as you overflow with my fullness, they will be able to see who I truly am and will find themselves unexpectedly drawn to me. Show them the way into my throne room where they will receive their own revelation of my love for them and the path to being filled with all my fullness and flooded with my presence."

* Breathing Exercises:

1. *Write down Ephesians 3:19 from the Amplified Bible (found at the beginning of this section) onto a piece of paper or index card. Carry it around with you all week; meditate on it as you drive, brush your teeth, cook, take a 5-minute work break, etc. Ask the Lord to show you what this verse means for **you**.*

2. *Do you desire to become a body wholly filled and flooded with God Himself? Examine your heart for an honest answer. Do you want His presence to flood your entire being, disrupting your schedule, neatly managed life, methods of coping, relationships, idols, and the walls of control and safety that you hide behind? Are you ready to let go of these things and allow His mighty flood to wash them away and transform your life?*

If your answer is "yes," share this desire with Him. Ask Him for an experience of Ephesians 3:19. Share the desire of your heart with Him and listen to any words He may want to share back.

If your answer is "no," seek to identify the reason. Talk to the Lord honestly about where you are at. Ask Him to meet you in this place and to show you the way forward so that you can one day invite His fullness to flood your life. He is incredibly patient and is happy to meet you where you are today. He isn't in a hurry and is happy to lead you step by step at whatever pace you need to go at.

Positioned

Okay, Lord, I've shared my longing for your fullness and you've shared your desire to fill me with it. Now how do we get there? What's the key?

"Beloved, everything you've been learning up till now is the key. The breathing exercises I've taken you through are the key. You can't make a flood happen, but what you *can* do is position yourself for a flood. If heavy rain is in the forecast (and let me tell you, it is!), any house in the flood zone *will* get flooded. Everything I have been teaching you up until now has been to get you in the flood zone: getting rooted by the stream and established securely in my love, traveling further up and further into the dimensions of my love, and seeking a revelation of it that surpasses knowledge. My child, I have led you through the process. I have shown you the way to the flood zone. Just set up camp here and the flood of my fullness will come.

As you set-up camp, make room for my flood by continuing to soak in my love. For as you soak in my love, letting it penetrate every insecurity, fear, and wound in your heart, you will be able to let go of the control you cling to and the methods you use to try to fill the empty places within you. Then you will finally be an open and free vessel that I can enter, take over, and flood with my very fullness

Notice Paul says, *"That you may be filled"*[1] not *"that you may fill yourselves."* I do the filling—not you. So be free. There's no pressure for you to try to fill yourself with my love, joy, peace, or anything else. I will fill you with them—your only job is to stay empty (not trying to fill yourself with other things) and soak in my love and presence. Rest in my love. And then trust that as you remain in my love, I *will* fill you to the measure with all the fullness that I am. There is no striving in this process, only restful receiving.

Remember that in the natural world, floods come in different ways. Sometimes they come with torrential downpours. Sometimes they come with consistent rain for weeks at a time—the rain may not be extremely heavy, but its consistency creates a flood. It is the same in the spiritual world as I flood you with my fullness. Sometimes I will flood you with torrential downpours of my Spirit as you spend time in my presence and open yourself up to me. Other times, the filling will be gradual as I consistently pour out my fullness while you walk in receptive expectation and trust throughout the day. Be open to all of my methods. Be receptive and thankful for however my fullness comes. Don't try to fit my filling work into a box. It won't always look like what you'd expect, but I guarantee it will always be uniquely wonderful! My flooding will look different throughout the days and years of your own life, and it will look different in the lives of each of my children. Don't worry about that—just be open and receptive!

I will warn you though that in whatever method it comes, the flood of my fullness is going to disrupt your day. It won't be orderly—no flood is. You can't just have a little of my fullness flood into one area of your heart—it will take over everything. It will disrupt your schedule. But let it, Beloved! Just receive

---

[1] Ephesians 3:19b

and let me fill you to overflowing. I will fill you with the most refreshing, life-giving water you can ever imagine. Don't cling to what's familiar and comfortable. Let me disrupt your neatly managed world and fill you with a fullness you didn't know existed. Ask and you will receive, seek and you shall find, knock and the door will be opened to you.[2] I am telling you right now that you will be a vessel wholly filled and flooded with my very presence. I am committed to seeing you through to this end with all my heart. I, who have called you, am faithful, and I will do it.[3] It is I who began this good work in you who will carry it on to completion.[4] So surrender, sit back, and enjoy the ride.

No Breathing Exercises, Beloved! Today, rest in the fact that you have been positioning yourself for a flood through all the previous breathing exercises and that it is I who will fill you! You don't have to do anything to fill yourself. Don't even try. Just rest in my promises and faithfulness today. I will complete the work I began in you. Smile and enjoy your day in peace."

---

[2] Matthew 7:7
[3] 1 Thessalonians 5:24
[4] Philippians 1:6

FULLY MORE

"Now to him who is able to do immeasurably more than all we ask or imagine, according to his power that is at work within us . . ." Ephesians 3:20

I AM Able

"Beloved, it is with great joy that I invite you into a deeper understanding of my boundless ability. I am able to do infinitely more than you could ever imagine or ask. *Nothing* is too hard for me. If I spoke the world into existence, designed every molecule and cell in your body, and hold the galaxies in the palm of my hand, don't you think I am able to do everything else you could possibly dream of? Whatever the task, it's nothing for me; it's not even close to being difficult. Because I AM God. I say the word and it will be done. I am seated on the throne above every rule and authority and what I speak will be accomplished. No other power can stand up to me. Beloved, I want to reveal my power and might to you and this revelation will change the way you see the problems around you, the circumstances you live in, and every encounter you have throughout the day. Whatever problem you face, I am bigger and I am able. There is nothing to fear, nothing to be discouraged about, no reason to be anxious or worried. For I, your God, am able.

Picture a little girl trying and trying to tie her shoelaces and finally giving up, announcing that the task is "too hard." When her father asks what's wrong, she tells him about the impossible task before her.

"I can help you with that, you know," the Father says. "I know how to tie shoes very well."

"Oh no Daddy, I don't think you understand how hard it really is and I already tried for 20 minutes. I don't think you'll be able to help me."

The father replies, "My child, I have been tying shoes for the past 30 years and I can assure you that I'm quite good at it. Let me show you."

And the Father stoops down to tie his daughter's shoes and she sits back amazed.

My child, do you realize that this is what your problems are like for me? I know they seem impossible, complicated, and unsolvable to you, but they're really nothing for me. They're like tying a shoelace.

But I want you to do more than believe that I am able. I also long for you to believe that I'm willing. There are many times you believe that I'm able to do something for you, but you don't trust that I'm willing. You don't trust my willing heart towards you. So I am telling you today—I am willing. Beloved, I will tell you again and again, as many times as you need to hear it. My heart is generous towards you. I am *for* you, and I am willing. It's who I am. I am a willing God: willing to heal[1], willing to give[2], willing to intervene[3], willing to forgive[4], willing to provide[5], willing to meet your needs[6]. I am willing to change my mind at the request of one of my children[7], willing to grant

---

[1] Luke 5:12-13
[2] Matthew 7:7-11
[3] John 2:1-11
[4] Matthew 9:1-8
[5] Luke 9:10-17
[6] Philippians 4:19
[7] Genesis 18:20-33

you the request of your lips[8] and willing to give you the desires of your heart.[9] I am willing; I want to and I will! I am *for* you, Beloved, and I am more able and willing than you have ever imagined."

[8] John 16:24
[9] Psalm 37:4

* Breathing Exercises:

1. *Do you believe God is truly able? Is there an area of your life in which you struggle to trust His ability? What situation seems too impossible for Him to heal or fix? Spend some time meditating on His strength, might, and abilities. As you do, ask Him to show you how small this problem is to Him, how easy it is to solve and redeem. Surrender this area to the Lord and ask for His help!*

2. *Do you believe God is willing? Maybe you believe He is able, but struggle to trust that He's willing to intervene on your behalf. Share this struggle with Him and ask Him to speak into your doubts. Then listen. Let Him share about His constant willingness to work on your behalf and to bless you. Look up the scriptures in the footnotes of this section. Believe His words. Rest in them throughout the rest of this week. Your God is more than able—He is willing! He **delights** to come through for you.*

Immeasurably More

"Beloved, there is still so much for you to discover about the extent of my goodness, power, and intentions toward you. There is much more to my character and nature than you currently see. What you think you know of me only scratches the surface of who I truly am, the magnitude of my love for you, and the things I have in store for you—all of this is infinitely greater than you have ever imagined. There are things about my goodness, character, and plans for you that are beyond your realm of comprehension. Your finite mind hasn't dared to dream at the level of abundance that characterizes my heart for you.

In some ways, your dreams are like those of the lost boys of Sudan who sustained themselves for years by eating mud and drinking their own urine as they fled the war in their country. To them, a simple plate of rice and beans would have been extravagant, an incredible gift compared to the mud and urine they were accustomed to. Their experience hadn't offered them knowledge about grander delicacies than rice to dream about.

But, what if the President of the United States took a few of those boys and brought them to America to spend Christmas in the White House? Even their largest dreams and imaginations wouldn't be able to prepare them for the mansion and feast awaiting them. These boys would enter a banquet hall with gourmet delicacies they never knew existed. The variety and quantity of food would be more than they could imagine. From their past experience in Sudan, where a feast was a fifty pound bag of rice divided among two hundred refugees, there is no way they could have imagined this much food available in one place at one time.

Beloved, in a way this is what it's like with you. You have trouble daring to believe for a plate of rice and beans, when actually I want to bless you with a feast at the White House with gifts and foods you don't even know exist. And I want to bless others through you in the same way.

My child, I desire to bring immeasurably more into your life than you could possibly imagine. Not just a little bit more, but infinitely, abundantly more. You can dream as big as your mind and heart are capable of, but my goodness and what I have in store for you is still infinitely greater. This is true for the gifts I want to give *to* you, as well as the things I want to do *through* you. I long to give you gifts of joy, peace, security, love, and provision that are infinitely greater than what you've dreamed of. And I want to work through you in ways you haven't dared to imagine yet: healings, casting out demons, words of knowledge and prophecy for people, and so much more! Yes, I want to do these things through you! These miracles aren't just for special people, or for my followers long ago; I desire to display my miraculous love and power through all of my children. Remember what Jesus said as he was preparing the disciples for his death and resurrection?

*"I tell you the truth, **anyone** who has faith in me will do what I have been doing. He will do even greater things than these, because I am going to the Father. And I will do whatever you ask in my name, so that the Son may bring glory to the Father. You may ask me for anything in my name, and I will do it."*
—John 14:12-14

Beloved, "anyone" means *you*. I long for you to step out in faith, trusting that I want to do even greater things through you than I did in Jesus' life. All authority in heaven and on earth is mine and I delight to use that authority to answer your prayers for miracles. Just start asking me! Take me out of the box you've put me in and take your faith and dreams out of the box you've put them in. Beloved, it's time to follow me into the "immeasurably more."

* Breathing Exercises:

1. *Do you believe the Lord wants to give you immeasurably more than all you can ask or imagine? Do you believe He wants to do more through your life than you can imagine? If you have doubts about either of these areas, bring them to the Lord. Talk to Him about your doubts or confusion and ask Him to show you the truth.*
2. *Think back on one situation in your life where God did immeasurably more than you could have asked or imagined. Thank Him for this gift and then share the story with at least one person this week. We need to tell our stories to remind ourselves and others of the mighty, extravagant God we serve. If others are struggling to believe God for the immeasurably more in their own lives, it will strengthen their faith to hear your testimony. They can draw encouragement from your story as you remind them of the nature and power of God who loves to work on behalf of His children.*

The Dare

"You do not have, because you do not ask God. When you ask, you do not receive because you ask with wrong motives, that you may spend what you get on your pleasures." James 4:2b-3

"Beloved, part of the reason that you're not living in my "immeasurably more" is that you're not daring to ask me for big things. So today, I dare you to start asking big. I dare you to imagine the greatest and grandest things possible about me, your future and what I want to do through you. I dare you to ask and dream to the greatest extent that your imagination can take you and then I'm going to show you how much greater I am than even your wildest dreams. *"For my thoughts are not your thoughts, neither are your ways my ways. As the heavens are higher than the earth, so are my ways higher than your ways and my thoughts than your thoughts."*[1]

Your requests of me are so small. Their smallness actually insults me. The size of your requests show the small God you believe me to be and the stingy heart you believe I possess. The sad thing is that even when you bring your little requests to me, you don't ask for them with much faith. So often you ask me for something and then use all your human tactics to try to bring about the answer yourself—you don't really trust me to see to it. Beloved, I'm able *and* I'm willing—remember?

---

[1] Isaiah 55:8-9

Right now I want you to dream big. I dare you to dream as big as you possibly can. Dream for the Kingdom. Don't just dream for your own little kingdom—dream for *my* Kingdom! It's okay. I'm giving you permission to ask. I want you to ask me for big things—for God-sized miracles. It's time to start asking me for bigger things than the equivalent of "tying your shoes" for you. Yes, I can tie your shoes and I will continue to tie your shoes and teach you to tie your own shoes, but I have so much more that I want to give you and I want you to start asking.

This is fun for me. I love dreaming with my children. I love it when they have enough confidence in my nature, love, generosity, and power to ask me for *big* things. Their big requests bring me glory and honor. For in their asking of huge things, they are acknowledging me as the mighty, loving God that I am. They are declaring my nature. They are exalting me as the Almighty, Sovereign God, the King of Kings and Lord of Lords. Go ahead, dream and ask big right now. Don't worry about analyzing if each dream is from me or not, or if it is my will for you. I want you to practice asking me for God-sized requests. I want to stretch and exercise your imagination and level of expectation. Know that this is an act of worship, for you are approaching me and acknowledging me as the God that I truly am."

* Breathing Exercises:

1. *Schedule a dreaming date with the Lord this week. You can go on a walk, sit at a coffee shop, picnic in the park, or go to the beach. Ask Him to dream and imagine with you. Allow yourself to dream big! Allow Him to pull up past dreams that have been buried in your heart. Ask for a revelation of His dreams for you. He has incredible, God-sized dreams for you, so dream with Him! Let your imagination go. Let your creativity flow.*

2. *After you dream with the Lord, dare to ASK for the fulfillment of those dreams. Bring your dreams and requests to the One who believes in you more than you can possibly imagine. Bring them to the One who is more committed to your future and good than even you are. Ask Him for the "immeasurably more!" Let this be your act of worship as your requests proclaim His greatness and goodness!*

The Dance

"I am the vine; you are the branches. If a man remains in me and I in him, he will bear much fruit; apart from me you can do nothing." John 15:5

"Not by might nor by power, but by my Spirit, says the Lord Almighty." Zechariah 4:6b

"Beloved, as I bring the "immeasurably more" into and through your life, you must understand that it will never come by your own strength or power. The things that come from your own strength are the things that *you* can imagine. But the things that you can't begin to ask or imagine are things that can only come through *my* power. You walk around with such pressure on your shoulders, feeling it's your responsibility to create the "immeasurably more" in situations. You carry the weight of feeling like it's *you* who needs to deliver the life-changing message at church, *you* who needs to get a prophetic word for someone, *you* who needs to heal the sick, *you* who needs to save Africa, *you* who needs to orchestrate getting together with your husband . . . and the list goes on and on. My child, I'm inviting you to rest now from all this pressure. None of this should be on your shoulders. Yes, I want to do these things through you, but I will provide the power; you just get to be the vessel. The pressure's off.

It doesn't matter how hard you work, your striving will never produce the "immeasurably more." You can produce "pretty good," and things that outwardly look impressive, but really, all

209

those things don't amount to much of anything. If my power isn't behind them, they won't have lasting, life-giving impact. It's like I told you in John 15:5, "apart from me, you can do *nothing*." It's only through remaining in me that you will produce true, life-giving fruit that will last. No more stressing about getting a prophetic word for someone or giving an amazing talk. You just focus on staying connected to me and staying filled with my Spirit, and I will take care of the "immeasurably more" stuff.

Beloved, if you continue to strive to bear fruit for me in your own wisdom and strength, at the end of your life you will look back on a past of "pretty good" and sometimes "impressive" things. They may look good to an outsider and you may have lots of accolades and awards on your wall, but there won't be much eternal impact to any of them. I'm telling you that if you can learn to abide with me, staying completely connected to me throughout your day, you will be able to look back on a life filled with the "immeasurably more." When you learn to rely on my strength that is in you instead of your own, you'll begin to see me move in mighty ways through you. Beloved, I am in you and my power is in you. I know you don't fully trust that yet or trust me to come through, but I'm telling you it's true. Rest and trust in my abiding presence in you. I *will* do immeasurably more than all you can ask or imagine according to *my power* that is at work *within you!*"

Swing Dancing

As I listened to these words from the Lord, it reminded me of my swing dancing experience last week. I absolutely love swing dancing, but I'm definitely no pro at it. I took 12 weeks of lessons two years ago and have gone dancing about once a month since then. Though I can keep up pretty well on the floor, I'm much less advanced than the majority of the other dancers who grace the dance floor multiple evenings a week. And I'm extremely less advanced than Steve. I had never met Steve before, but I was mesmerized watching him dance around the floor. He was amazing!!! This guy had obviously been dancing for years and you could tell by the grin on his face that there was nothing he'd rather be doing.

About halfway through the night, Steve approached me to ask if I wanted to dance. You bet I did! Even though I knew I probably wouldn't be able to keep up with him, I couldn't pass up this opportunity to dance with such an amazing dancer. And boy was I ever glad I tried it! Even though I had no clue what I was doing, Steve was such an amazing leader that I suddenly found myself doing moves way beyond my wildest imagination, moves I didn't know I was capable of, moves I didn't know existed. I was miraculously spinning across the floor in ways I didn't know were possible. I was swing dancing at a whole new level in a league I didn't know was feasible for me, given my level of experience and small handbook of moves. But the thing was, it had nothing to do with me that night. It had nothing to do with my dancing ability, experience, or knowledge of the moves. It had everything to do with my incredible leader. He was such a perfect leader that I found myself spinning beautifully across the floor and jumping into the air at the exact moment he did, even though he never told me to jump or what move was coming next. As long as I focused on following his lead and staying connected to him and didn't think too hard about the steps, I found myself dancing beyond my wildest imagination. I got to live and dance in the "immeasurably more" that night because of his strength and ability to lead and to dance.

It's like this with God. I know that I will find myself living in the "immeasurably more" when I stop focusing on the steps and thinking so much, and abandon myself to this dance of trust with Him. He is an incredible dancer and leader and all I have to do is stay connected, keep eye contact, and follow! He wants to lead me into the "immeasurably more," but that means I have to follow. Too often, I want to lead my own moves. But with me in the lead, I'll never reach the "immeasurably more". I may reach the land of "pretty good," but that's as far as my own leading can take me. The little storehouse of moves that I can dream up is nothing compared to His. He's inviting me to take His hand, surrender the lead and control, and to get ready for the dance of my life—one beyond my wildest dreams and imaginations! Now that's an invitation that I don't want to miss.

* Breathing Exercises:

1. *Are you carrying pressure right now to make the immeasurably more happen in your life and the lives of others? The Lord wants you to be free from this pressure. **He** will take care of the "immeasurably more"—your job is to stay connected with Him and abide in Him throughout the day. Surrender the control and pressure you have been carrying. Ask Him to free you! It may help to reflect back over your life. Is it filled with moments of "immeasurably more," "pretty good," or some combination of both? Think about the "immeasurably more" moments. Who was responsible for them? Did they come from your own work and striving, or a miracle from God? What about the "pretty good" moments? As you reflect on this, allow yourself to rest in the truth that God is the only one who can work the immeasurably more in and through your life.*

2. *As you learn to let God lead this dance of life, you will unexpectedly find yourself living in the "immeasurably more." But you must let Him lead. Pick one exercise below to practice being a good dance follower this week:*

- *Don't look down at your feet. Keep eye contact with your leader (the Lord).*
- *Don't think too hard about the steps; just focus on staying connected to your leader.*
- *Don't try to lead the moves yourself—let Him lead and follow whatever step He leads.*
- *Don't worry if He starts leading a move you don't know. Just allow your body to respond to His nudges. Stay loose and responsive and you will end up automatically doing the move He leads.*

FULLY GLORIFIED

"To him be glory in the church and in Christ Jesus

throughout all generations, forever and ever! Amen."

Ephesians 3:21

His Glory

In the end, everything in life and everything we have been learning is about the glory of God. We were created to reflect His glory on earth and to join with all creation to see that He is fully glorified. Paul understands this and concludes his prayer in Ephesians 3 with a reminder that all of his petitions for the Ephesians are ultimately for God's glory. For as they enter into an experience of God's fullness, God will become famous! Paul doesn't pray for the sake of the Ephesians alone and his requests aren't for the glorification of the Ephesian church. They are so that the world will see the fullness, power, and love of God displayed in the Ephesian church and glorify *Him!* The ultimate goal is to see God fully glorified in all the earth through His radiant, overflowing Bride!

God will be glorified when we grasp the length, width, height, and depth of His love for us and enter into a "ginosko" understanding of this love that surpasses knowledge. For when we do, everything about our countenance and lives will reflect this all-consuming love. When we enter into an experience of the love for which we were created, the world will take notice and they will be drawn to the source of that love: the greatest Lover of all-time. John Piper sums it up best in his famous quote, "God is most glorified in us when we are most satisfied in Him."[1] It is so true: a radiant and overflowing Bride testifies to an incredible Bridegroom. Our fullness testifies to an all-sufficient, abundant, radically loving God!

---

[1] John Piper, *Let the Nations be Glad,* 31.

If we were to walk around genuinely joyful, overflowing, and secure in God's unending love—especially in the midst of frustrating or painful circumstances—what a testimony it would be to our incredible God. If our joy, confidence, and fullness is genuine (not just a show for others where we pretend to feel things we really don't), it is bound to draw others to God. They will recognize that what is going on with us is supernatural—something not of this world—and they'll want it. For how can the empty, the discouraged, and the unloved not want to know the God who has provided us with such fullness, hope, and love? When we let God truly be God in our lives: our adoring Father, our source of identity and fullness, the unconditional lover of our souls, and the one who wants to lead us into the "immeasurably more", the world will be drawn to Him and He will be fully glorified.

The world has such an inaccurate picture of who God is, often because of us, His followers. What kind of God do we portray when we walk around stressed out, worried, doubting, insecure, and hopeless? Obviously our God must not be very capable, trustworthy, or hopeful. *Oh Lord, please forgive me for all the times I portray this inaccurate picture of you because I'm caught up in myself, my circumstances, and my worries.*

When I think of glorifying God, I usually think of singing to Him during worship at church or going on a mission trip to serve others. But what if one of the greatest ways I can bring God glory is to simply let Him love me, let Him fill me to the measure with all His fullness, and then allow Him to do immeasurably more than all I can ask or imagine according to *His* power that is at work within me? What if my countenance is a stronger testimony to who He is than my words or actions? I'm beginning to believe this is true.

But a radiant countenance and supernatural fullness aren't something we can fake. People can tell when we're faking confidence and joy, and they can tell when it's genuine. The key to bringing God glory isn't putting on a happy face and lying to others about how great things are in God even though everything in our life is falling apart. That's not what people want to see or hear from us. They want to see something genuine; something true, lasting and real. And the good news is that the love, fullness, and power of God are the truest, most eternal realities there are. So the key is letting these realities become real for *us*. To soak in His love, meditate on these scriptures, and come into a heart knowledge of this love that surpasses mere head knowledge, until we naturally begin to overflow with His fullness. We simply need to learn to believe and enjoy His love. And the more we begin to receive this life-changing, world-shaking love, the more He will receive the glory due His name! The more famous He will become!

* Breathing Exercises:

1. *When you think about trying to bring glory to God, what actions usually come to mind? Do these feel like a light or heavy load to bear? How do you feel about this sentence:*

   *"What if one of the greatest ways I can bring God glory is to simply let Him love me, let Him fill me to the measure with all His fullness, and then allow Him to do immeasurably more than all I can ask or imagine according to **His** power that is at work within me?"*

   Talk to the Lord about this idea and ask Him to share His thoughts with you. Listen to any further revelation He may want to give you.

2. *Reflect back on your life throughout the weeks or months you have been reading this book. As God has been revealing His heart to you and leading you down the path to His fullness, can you see new ways that you have brought Him glory? Have others noticed a change in your countenance? Your peace? Your confidence? Ask the Lord to show you some of the ways that He is receiving glory through this journey. As He shows you, rejoice and celebrate these situations with Him!*

Throughout Eternity

As children of God, we have been given the incredible honor of participating in the anthem of His eternal glory! His word says that He will receive glory today through his church, throughout all generations in the future, and then forever and ever throughout eternity. This gives great significance to our days. As we bring Him glory through our lives, we are participating in the eternal story of His glory, in the one thing that will last. Most things in my life will cease one day: my job, my financial situation, my looks, my family, the things on my to-do-list, and even my very life on earth will come to an end. These things are like shifting winds; my own life is a mist.[1] However, God and his worship are eternal! And we get the privilege of playing a part in the eternal symphony of praise to Him!

I love that God desires to receive glory through the church, through His people. Creation glorifies God by testifying to His character and power. In nature we see God's creativity, majesty, wisdom, humor, and so much more. But nature isn't the only thing created to testify to His character and bring Him glory. We, His church, His Bride were created to do the same thing. Our lives, our attitudes, our fullness, our joy, and our love should all declare the greatness of our God.

But it doesn't just stop with us. God won't be fully glorified in our own lives and generation alone. He is to be glorified throughout *all* generations. So we must pass down the story

---

[1] James 4:14

of His greatness from generation to generation. The portrait of God that we pass down to our children is more important than anything else we do for them. Our lives, faith, peace, and joy should give our children a "radiant idea of who God is."[2] Remember, children can notice when we are faking; they are sensitive to the difference between what they are taught and the realities that they observe. If you teach them a Bible story about God's ability to provide, but then walk around distracted and worried about your own financial situation, your actions will speak louder to them about the nature of God than the story you read. But as you truly begin to walk in a heart revelation of the grandness of God's love and intentions towards you, you will overflow with His fullness and it will lavishly fall onto your children. Soon they will be as confident in His heart as you are and they too will overflow with His fullness, bringing Him radiant glory in this world. His glory will continue from generation to generation!

Yet, one day, the birth of new generations will cease as God brings an end to time and the earth as we know it. On that day, we will finally be free from these earthly bodies and the confinements of time, as He welcomes us into the realm of eternity that our hearts have always longed for.[3] We will finally be home! And as we enter the joys of eternity, of no longer fighting the clock and feeling like time is slipping through our fingers, we will join the joy-filled eternal worship of the King—worship that will continue forever and ever! Oh friends, the worship and glory we get to bring Him now is only a rehearsal for the real show coming—the one described in Revelation 7:9-10 where people from every tribe, tongue, and nation will gather before His throne, worshipping Him with the beauty

---

[2] A common phrase spoken by one of my favorite teachers, Graham Cooke.

[3] Ecclesiastes 3:11b

and diversity of the world. On that day when worshippers from every people group join before His throne to glorify the King, our great God will finally be *fully glorified*. And on that day as we enter His radiant presence and join with the worship of the nations, our fullness will finally be complete. And our fullness and His glory will continue in inexplicable joy forever and ever. Amen!

* Breathing Exercises:

1. *In what ways can you help pass down the testimony of God's greatness to future generations? Maybe it's the way you interact with your own children, or stories you share with children in your neighborhood or at your church. Ask the Lord to show you your role in furthering His glory throughout all generations into eternity!*
2. *Spend five minutes meditating on Revelation 7:9-10 and the eternity awaiting us—an eternity where our fullness and God's glory are finally complete! Sometimes it's good to take a few minutes to remember where we're going and what this whole life is leading up to.*

"After this I looked and there before me was a great multitude that no one could count, from every nation, tribe, people and language, standing before the throne and in front of the Lamb. They were wearing white robes and were holding palm branches in their hands. And they cried out in a loud voice: "Salvation belongs to our God, who sits on the throne, and to the Lamb."
Revelation 7:9-10

LIVING FULL

Struggle

I have to be honest, I wrestled with a lot of questions while writing this book—some of them may be questions you struggled with while reading it:

These words from God sound great and the scriptures seem hopeful, but are these promises really true?

Could all of this really be true about God's heart for me and for every person who reads this book?

Is a life of fullness beyond our wildest imaginations truly available to us?

Can these promises actually begin to play out in our hectic, messed-up lives?

I also wrestled with fear:

Lord, what if I don't hear you correctly and I misrepresent your heart to others? What if people misunderstand and take these words the wrong way?

What if I get to the end of this book and nothing in my life is different? What if I listen to your heart and work through the breathing exercises, but still don't seem to experience the fullness you're talking about? And what if I lead others down a dead-end road with all of this? Honestly, even though all the things you've told me throughout the book sound amazing and wonderful, I have a hard time picturing my life being characterized by many of them.

I wrestled with God, with haunting questions and fear, but I'm so thankful for the journey. I've been reminded throughout the process that it's okay to struggle with God. Relationship and intimacy with Him requires struggle. He is God and I'm a human. His thoughts and ways are so much higher than mine and it won't always be easy to understand Him, believe His words, learn to hear Him, and begin to think like He thinks. But He understands all this and He loves the struggle because it means we are seeking Him and entering deeper into relationship with Him.

In the Old Testament, God named His chosen people, Israel, which means "people who struggle with God." I find that fascinating. If I were God and were going to name my chosen people, I think I would have named them "My Beloved," or, "Joy of My Heart," or something like that. But He names them "People who Struggle with God." He knew that His relationship with them would be marked with struggle, but He chose them anyway. So I've now come to see the name Israel as a term of endearment. The fact that they would struggle with Him meant that they were living in relationship with Him. They were truly His people. The other nations wouldn't struggle with Him because they could care less about Him and weren't in relationship with Him. But those that struggled with Him, His precious Israel, those were the ones close to His heart and learning to navigate this awesome relationship with the King of Kings.

I love this! I love that it's okay to struggle with God. I love that He's okay with it. I love that it means that I'm one of His beloved children, moving deeper into His heart and into intimacy with Him. As you might have guessed if you read the author bio on the back of this book, God brought my Prince Charming throughout the process of writing this book! Michael Joseph Blaser is such an incredible gift from God, a man far beyond my wildest dreams. And though our first year of marriage has been amazing, we have also struggled at times. But that's simply because we're two different people learning to become one, and that will always bring struggle. We struggle because we're growing in intimacy together. It's beautiful and I wouldn't change it for anything. The same is true for my relationship with God. As we grow in intimacy, we struggle, and it's beautiful!

So if you've struggled throughout parts of this book, that's great! It means you're actually digesting the words instead of skimming over them, and God's Kingdom thinking is confronting your earthly thinking. Feel the freedom God gives you in this process. He's okay with the fact that some of these words might take a while for you to fully believe. He is patient and kind and will be with you through the journey.

As for me, I can honestly say that my heart is at peace now. God has answered my questions, silenced my fears, and assured me that He has indeed been involved in each page of this book. This *is* His heart and the words throughout these pages *were* from Him. They were His words to me, and I can trust them. And though every word may not specifically apply to every situation in your own life, these words do represent His heart toward you as well, for they represent His unchanging nature.

And I no longer fear that this is a dead-end road, for throughout the three-year journey of writing this book, fullness has actually begun to consume and characterize my life. I see it now! God's words have not come back void. Though I am still on a journey, I have more and more days in which I find myself overflowing with the fullness of God. It's amazing! There are many days that I still get sucked into the world of worries and distractions and completely miss His fullness, but then there are the days when I "get it." And those days have been so exciting! Those days, I'm beginning to realize what it means to be fully alive and to walk in the joyful fullness of God. I'm stepping into the life He created me for.

So as I end this book, my heart overflows with hope for you! As I now share some of my recent experiences with fullness and the practical ways it's beginning to play out in my daily life, I pray the stories give you hope for your own journey. I pray they encourage you to hang in there and to continue to soak in these scriptures and spend time practicing the breathing exercises, because it's worth it. Trust me! It's worth throwing yourself into this pursuit towards understanding the heart of your Heavenly Father.

I pray that you are encouraged by these stories. But remember that these are just my stories. You will have your own stories. God's fullness will manifest itself differently in your life—and that's wonderful! It expresses itself uniquely through different personalities. But the joyful truth is that it *will* begin to display itself in your life and you *will* have your own stories to share. You *will* be filled to the measure with all the fullness of God and that *will* play out practically in your daily life.

* Breathing Exercises:

1. *Have you wrestled with some of the questions at the beginning of this reading? Are you still struggling with some of them? It's okay! Rest in that freedom today. Know that God delights in the struggle that takes you deeper into intimacy with Him. Ask the Lord to speak into your lingering questions and fears, and allow yourself to enjoy this process.*

2. *Are there ways you have begun to see your life change as you have read this book? Do you see areas of your life where God's fullness is beginning to bring transformation? Have you had moments of experiencing the reality of His fullness in your day? Thank Him for these moments and ask Him to reveal other ones to you that you may not have noticed.*

Kenya

As I boarded the plane to begin my annual trip to Kenya, I wondered what my summer there would hold. I was traveling to a place that had become my second home after spending many summers there with Empowering Lives International. I looked forward to settling into village life once again and reconnecting with my friends and "family" there. But my heart held many questions as I flew this time. Would this trip be different? After writing about fullness for two years and soaking in the truths of God's heart for me, would those things actually play out in the way I lived and ministered there? I prayed they would. I prayed that I would find myself singing from my "core" instead of my "throat." I prayed that my usual striving there would be replaced by a peaceful abiding that allowed God's fullness to fill and overflow out of me.

God sent me my first confirmation that indeed this trip would be different through an e-mail I received my first day in Kenya. It was from a dear friend and prayer warrior:

"Kierra, I once heard our bishop share about his desire to be soaked in the Holy Spirit like a sponge soaked in water. A dry sponge can only soak up whatever's around them (good and bad). But he wanted to be a wet, Holy Spirit soaked sponge, dripping puddles of blessings wherever he went.

May this time with God in Kenya be a time for you to "soak" in His Spirit. As I prayed for you, I saw you running and walking the dirt roads of Africa dripping puddles of blessings along the way. I'm not sure the significance, but I saw the water that dripped off your hand sprinkle onto the side of the road. All of a sudden TALL stalks of corn bearing HUGE fruit appeared. As you drip these puddles of blessings, may God use them to nurture seeds that have already been planted."

Linda's words encouraged me so much. I longed to be a Holy Spirit soaked sponge dripping God's blessings wherever I went. That's what fullness is all about! And that's where true fruit comes from. I held onto these words and to the lessons I had been learning through my breathing exercises and was amazed to see the difference they made as I started ministry in the village.

In past summers there, I would race around from one thing to the next, trying to cram my day with as much ministry as possible. I was always working and always a bit stressed. My first summer there, one of my Kenyan friends said to me, "Kierra, you are ever working. I don't even think you know who you are because you never stop working. You don't have time to know who you are." She was right. Her words hit hard. I didn't have time to know who I truly was or who God truly was. But I didn't know at that time how to slow down and sing from my core instead of my throat.

But this trip, I felt so free from all of that striving and hurriedness. I was free to spend four hours enjoying the Lord at the gazebo by the river. I had no need to prove anything or to impress anyone. I didn't feel the usual inner pressure to be "working" all the time or accomplishing things. I was free to soak and to let Him fill me and then overflow out of me. My heart was at peace. And you know what? My ministry became much deeper and more impactful. When I was with people, I was actually fully present to them. I came into meetings and relationships full, rested, and covered by God's spirit and presence. As I sat with my friends in their huts, I wasn't distracted by my normal worries or thoughts. I wasn't needy. I could hear God's heart and words for them. I was peaceful. And that peace transferred to them. One of my Kenyan friends commented about it one day.

He looked at me and said, "Kierra, I see hope in you. I see hope and happiness and life. I look at you and just see smiles."

"Do I seem different than last year?" I asked with curiosity.

"Yes. Last year you seemed stressed. But now I look at you and I just see life."

I couldn't believe it. God's fullness was overflowing out of me to the point where others were beginning to notice! I smiled and began to share with William what God had been teaching me about life to full and being filled to the measure with His fullness.

That entire summer was filled with divine moments like this where the fullness of God would bubble up out of me and begin to spill into my conversations and interactions with others. It was such a joy to watch Him work and invite others into life that is truly life. I continued to soak in Him and enjoy time with Him and He continued to overflow His fullness onto those around me.

* Breathing Exercises:

1. *Take some time to reflect on any ministry that you're involved in. It could be service at your church, activities in your community, ministry to your children or spouse, ministry to your co-workers—anywhere you are trying to serve the Lord and advance His Kingdom. Are you*

serving out of God's overflow, or out of your own strength? Are you singing from your throat or from your core? Are you trying to cram too many "good things" into your schedule, or are you letting the Lord guide your involvement? Talk to the Lord about what you would like to see change in the way you minister. Listen to His suggestions. Talk with Him about what it would look like to minister out of fullness. Let Him show you that picture and any steps you need to take to get there.

2. *Are you an overflowing sponge dripping blessings wherever you go? Or are you dry and soaking up whatever is around you (whether good or bad)? Spend some time soaking in God's presence and love this week, asking Him to make you that dripping wet sponge. Enjoy your time with Him!*

The Coffee Shop

It was three months ago that I saw him. He was working behind the counter at a coffee shop where I was reading one afternoon. I had a book in front of my face, but I couldn't read. I was too intrigued; too curious; too inspired. I had found someone who radiated fullness. After writing about it for three years, I felt like I was finally watching it in all its joyful glory. It was real, it was flowing out of him, and it was touching lives. He worked with a smile on his face. Not a fake smile, but a genuine one that seemed to well up from something deep inside of him and twinkled in his eyes. It was contagious. As people approached the counter to order and began to interact with him, they began to smile as well. They seemed to relax. The worries of life seemed to lighten off their shoulders. As he cracked good-humored jokes, they laughed. He put them at ease.

But it was more than his smile that touched them; it was his love. Unfiltered acceptance poured out of him for each person who walked through the door. It didn't matter their gender, race, clothing, or temperament; he greeted each person with uninhibited joy. It was like they just made his day by walking in. He bantered easily with them, asking about their family, school, etc. It seemed he knew many of them and the details of their lives. I could tell that each person who walked through the door felt loved and valued. I was fascinated to watch people linger at the counter even after they received their drinks. They wanted to hang out near him. His fullness and joy were contagious. He had something that people were hungry for. Even if they couldn't articulate it, I could tell that they hungered for it and wanted to be near it.

I didn't need to ask him if he was a Believer. I just knew. The love, joy, and fullness of God overflowed out of him so powerfully that there was no question in my mind. Only God could make someone glow that brightly. Only God could fill someone so fully. What a ministry that guy had. What a difference the fullness of God makes in ministry. He didn't have to psyche himself up to try to share his testimony with someone, or to ask them if they knew where they were going when they died. He didn't have to strive to do anything. He just let the fullness of God flow freely through him and people were drawn to it. I bet if anyone asked him what it was that made him so joyful (and I'm sure people ask him because I wasn't the only curious onlooker that day), he could share about the love of God to a very captive and open audience. People could tell it was genuine and I believe very few people that day would have written him off if he started talking about the joy of the Lord. There was no denying that he had something real and not of this world.

I left the coffee shop full and inspired that day. His fullness rubbed off on me. I left smiling and encouraged, seeing what fullness in ministry can look like. This is the kind of ministry that I want— ministry where God just overflows out of me throughout the day, drawing others to Himself and opening doors of conversation. I pray the Lord will continue to lead me to this place.

* Breathing Exercises:

1. *Do you know anyone like this? Someone who seems to naturally radiate God's fullness and love, peaking the curiosity of you and others? If you can think of someone like this, shoot them an e-mail or give them a call this*

week and ask them what their secret is. Tell them what you notice about them and ask them where it comes from and how they stay filled with it. Learn from the insights they share with you!

2. *Do you find yourself living like this guy? If not, what keeps you from living life like him? Is it fear of what others will think of you? Busyness? Preoccupation with worries? Ask the Lord to show you some of the hindrances that keep you from overflowing with His fullness. Ask for His wisdom to know how to break those hindrances and then take the first step that He shows you.*

The Gym

A few weeks after my experience at the coffee shop I had another encounter with fullness, but this time, to my great surprise and delight, I found that it was overflowing out of *me*! I think I assumed that I would suddenly wake up one day with the realization that I was finally overflowing with the fullness of God. I thought it would be obvious to me. But it didn't happen like that at all. It was such a gradual process of the Lord slowly filling me that I didn't even realize it was happening. Just like a steady rain over many days will begin to flood a home, the Lord had slowly but steadily been flooding me with His presence. And then one day at the gym, He opened my eyes to the work He had been doing.

I walked into the gym and greeted John, the guy who always sits at the welcome desk. I've never said more than a few words to him before, but this day he stopped me.

"Why are you always smiling when you come in here?" he asked. Surprised by his question, I stumbled to think of an answer. "I guess I just like working out," I lamely answered. "Oh," he said, and I continued up the stairs to my aerobics class.

All throughout my class, I thought about his comment. Was I really always smiling when I walked into the gym? If I was, it wasn't because I like working out. I do like exercising, but not enough to make me involuntarily smile throughout my time there. No, I was smiling and joyful because of God. I was definitely beginning to get a revelation of His love, and His contagious joy was filling me. I was beginning to experience His fullness! He was the source of my joy and I guess it was starting to show.

Someone had noticed God's fullness in me and had been intrigued enough to ask about it, and I hadn't been prepared to explain it to them. I felt terrible. I wanted a re-do. I didn't see John again for a few weeks, but when I finally did, I was ready to give him a better answer.

"Hey John," I called out as I walked over to him. "I've been wanting to talk to you. A few weeks ago, you asked me why I was always smiling. I told you it's because I like working out. But that's not the real reason."

"It's not?" he asked, a bit confused.

"No," I smiled. "It's because of my relationship with God. I've been getting to know Him more these past months, and the more I get to know Him and how much He loves me, the more joy I get. He is extremely joyful and His joy just spreads to me as I spend time with Him. He has been bringing the smile to my face."

I could tell that John was surprised, but a little intrigued and we began to talk about God and the Bible and both of our backgrounds. We chatted for a little bit and I know that I left him with something intriguing to chew on. He got to see a new side of the distant God he thought was out there and I left excited. God's fullness was beginning to spread!

* Breathing Exercises:

1. *By this time in your reading, I imagine that you too are beginning to overflow with some of God's fullness. Are you prepared to give an answer to people who begin to ask about it? Whether you believe it or not right now, people are going to notice God's fullness in you and ask you about it. Spend some time with the Lord thinking about how you would answer them. Don't be caught off-guard like I was and miss an opportunity to share the amazing work He's doing in you. Ask the Lord for opportunities to share with others and prepare your heart to be bold when those opportunities arise.*

2. *If someone has questioned you in the past about your joy, peace, countenance, etc . . . and you didn't give them the true or full answer, don't be afraid to go back to them with the truth. You might feel silly, but your words may be just what their hungering hearts are longing for.*

"Always be prepared to give an answer to everyone who asks you to give the reason for the hope that you have."
1 Peter 3:15b

The Post Office

It happened again a month later, this time at the post office. And this time, I was ready to give a correct explanation for the hope that I have and the fullness flowing through me.

The post office is just down the block from my office and I have frequented it often throughout the past four years. I always volunteer to take the mail there or pick up a package because it's a great excuse to get some fresh air and stretch my legs in the middle of a long work day. All the postal workers know me, or at least recognize me when I walk through the door, and I know most of them. I've tried to reach out to a few of them and share the love of God, but nothing really significant has happened through my efforts—at least nothing that I have been able to see.

Until last week. As I waited in line, I wondered which teller God would pair me up with. There was one lady who had served me a lot lately and I wondered if it would be her. I didn't know much about her, but I sensed pain and loneliness in her eyes. Sure enough, when I got to the front of the line, her register opened up and she called me over. I smiled and engaged in small talk with her as she rang up my packages. I was just getting ready to walk away when she looked at me and said, "What is it about you? Why are you always so happy when you come in here?"

I smiled and told her directly, "It's God. What you see is His joy in me. He is a God of amazing joy and love and the more I get to know Him, the more I get filled with His joy. It just rubs off on me."

She seemed a bit taken aback by my answer. But after thinking for a moment, she said, "Well, it shows. I see it in your face when you come in here."

I responded, "It's only God. This is a tough world with a lot of pain in it and I think our only hope for true joy is found in God and understanding how much He loves us and wants to walk this journey with us."

She gave a half smile and said, "Yeah, it's definitely a tough world."

I saw the pain in her eyes and said, "Yes it is, but I want you to know that God really loves you."

Tears filled her eyes and she looked away embarrassed. I didn't want to embarrass her more or hold the line up, so I told her goodbye and left it at that, knowing that I could continue to pray for her and share more in the future.

I walked back to our office rejoicing and thanking our faithful God. Another person had actually seen His fullness bubbling out of me and was now hopefully closer to knowing Him herself! I'm living in the flood zone—allowing Him to fill me to the measure with His fullness—and strangers are starting to notice. They really are drawn to it, curious about it, and hungry enough to ask about it. All that I've been writing about and pondering for the past three years is true and beginning to shine forth in my life. Praise God! I felt so alive as I drove home that evening. This is the life I was created for. This is who God created me to be: a daughter who is deeply in love with Him, secure in His love, and overflowing with His very presence. I love it!

This was so much better than going out on an assignment to share my faith with one person that day. I've been given assignments like that before, and while God may use them, they always feel a bit forced and unnatural to me. I feel awkward and I think the other person often feels awkward. But this—this living out of fullness and letting it draw others to God—this was fun! This felt natural. This felt authentic and real. I wasn't trying to produce fruit on my own. I was simply abiding in God and letting Him produce fruit through me. I felt so free, free to just be me! There was no pressure, simply the freedom to allow God to shine out of me in all of His glorious fullness.

I went on a walk that evening and couldn't stop smiling as I walked and thanked God for the day and for His fullness. I prayed, sang, and communed with Him as I walked. I was in my own little world with the Lord, not even thinking what I must look like to people I passed on the street. Suddenly I noticed a guy riding toward me on a bicycle. He was watching me. I smiled as he passed by, a bit embarrassed that he had caught me singing and talking to myself with a goofy grin on my face. Then to my great surprise, he looped around and started biking next to me, asking what I was up to. I had to smile as I realized that another person had seen the fullness of God overflowing in me, and was curious enough to turn around on his bike to find out more. I think he knew I wasn't crazy, but saw an unfiltered joy in me that you rarely see when passing people on the street. We talked for a bit and then he went off on his way. I continued on my walk with my goofy grin, thinking, *Lord, I could get addicted to this. This is so much fun and so easy. The years of getting to this point where I'm truly experiencing your fullness weren't easy, but now that I'm beginning to live in it, sharing about you to others is really effortless!*

I don't tell you these stories to toot my own horn or to try to sound like some spiritual giant. I tell them to encourage you.

I'm simply a stumbling girl who is fighting my way through doubts, perfectionism, and preconceived notions about God, trying to grasp the incredible dimensions of His love for me and the goodness of His heart. As I fight, listen to Him, and learn to breathe, He is leading me into the fullness we were each created for: the life abundant He came to give us. I still miss it many days, but I am slowly experiencing moments and hours of His fullness that are taking my breath away and making me so excited about this adventure called life.

I believe that God has this abundant life waiting for you as well. It doesn't matter your personality, age, race, or gender. Maybe you're the quiet type who is shy around strangers and uncomfortable talking to them. That's okay. God's fullness is still going to spill out of you and draw others to Him. It may not happen like it has for me, but it will happen in a way unique to you. As God fills you with His fullness, you may be filled with a deep peace and confidence that others take notice of. Even if you don't say anything to them, they may see it in your eyes or in the peaceful way you interact with your children. Maybe they will see it in your integrity or bravery or gentle calm. I don't know, but I do know that as you get a revelation of God's heart for you, He *will* fill you to the measure with His fullness and the world *will* be drawn to Him through you. You *will* begin to step into the immeasurably more.

I leave you with this encouragement:

There is no certain way this is all supposed to look. There is nothing that you have to "do." No pressure to "do" anything to try to get closer to God or to please Him more. No assignment to share your testimony with three people this week, or to participate in another service project, or to join a committee at church. Simply enjoy the King. Enjoy His love, trust His heart towards you, and let Him fill you to overflowing. He will do it, Beloved. He will fill you with His fullness, draw others to Himself, and lead you into the abundant life He created you for. Enjoy the ride!

No more breathing exercises. Simply enjoy the King, His freedom, and this incredible journey with Him!

CPSIA information can be obtained at www.ICGtesting.com
Printed in the USA
LVOW040735280112

265906LV00001B/3/P